P9-CQJ-048

MOULDERS OF NATIONAL DESTINIES

Wide World Photos, Inc.

THOMAS MASARYK

MOULDERS OF NATIONAL DESTINIES

By

F. H. SOWARD
B.A. (*Toronto*), B.Litt. (*Oxon.*)
Professor of History, University of British Columbia

OXFORD UNIVERSITY PRESS
London Toronto New York
1939

Second Edition, 1939

Printed in Canada

PREFACE TO THE SECOND EDITION

IN this revised and enlarged edition I have added essays on President Roosevelt, Prime Minister Neville Chamberlain and Mr. Anthony Eden which, like their predecessors, were first prepared as radio talks for the Canadian Broadcasting Corporation. To its officials I am further indebted for permission to utilize this material. My thanks are also due to Miss Anne Smith, reference librarian of the University of British Columbia, for her skill and tireless energy in uncovering source material, and to Miss Eva Morley for ungrudging and efficient stenographic assistance. In such stormy times the biographer of contemporary statesmen can do little more than run panting along, pen in hand, at the heels of his subject. However, I hope that the additional material covering the events of the eighteen months since the first preface was written may prove of use in understanding the news behind the headlines.

F. H. SOWARD

THE UNIVERSITY OF BRITISH COLUMBIA,
October, 1939.

PREFACE TO THE FIRST EDITION

THESE brief biographical sketches were originally prepared and delivered at the request of the Canadian Broadcasting Corporation to whom the author is indebted for permission to publish them. A few were also published in the *B. C. Teacher,* whose editor has likewise consented to their appearance in this book. Except for minor modifications, necessitated by the passage of time, they have been published in their original form. The author by no means believes in what has been called the "Great Man" theory of history, but recognizes that the quarter-century since the coming of the World War has afforded exceptional opportunities for strong-willed men devoted to a cause or a country to affect the lives and fortunes of millions. It is hoped that these attempts to describe concisely the upbringing and theories of almost a score of outstanding national heroes will make more intelligible their policies and more comprehensive the news of the day.

For permission to include the quotation from Emil Ludwig's *Nine Etched from Life* in the sketch of Briand, grateful acknowledgement is made to the author and to the publishers, Robert M. McBride & Company.

F. H. SOWARD

THE UNIVERSITY OF BRITISH COLUMBIA,
May, 1938.

CONTENTS

ILLUSTRATIONS

I

WOODROW WILSON AND THE STRUGGLE FOR A NEW WORLD ORDER

WOODROW Wilson, 28th President of the United States of America, was a man who, like Moses, could not lead his people into the Promised Land.

We have yet to read a well-rounded life of Wilson which will separate the man from the myth. His official biographer, R. S. Baker, estimates that there are five tons of documents alone about his career and has written the longest biography in the English language (eight volumes) covering his hero's career to the close of the World War. Both in life and after death the man has aroused intense admiration or violent dislike. Lord Charnwood, who wrote so admirable a life of Lincoln, wrote of Wilson, "In my eyes his singular and powerful figure appears an evil one which it may be right to pity but cannot be right to admire." In striking contrast the veteran Senator from Virginia, Carter Glass, once pounded on his desk until his knuckles bled while furiously denouncing Senator Nye and others who dared to impugn the honour and honesty of his hero.

Of Woodrow Wilson, Mr. Baker has said a little fancifully that he spent 54 years in preparing, ten years in living and three in dying. The years of preparation are often neglected but explain much about the man. Woodrow Wilson came of sturdy Scots and Ulster stock that emigrated to the United States in the early part of the nineteenth century. Canada has a link with his past in that his maternal grandfather, the Reverend Thomas Woodrow, settled first in Brockville as a Presbyterian minister but soon crossed the border in search of a larger congregation. Wilson was extremely proud of his Presbyterian preacher ancestry on both sides of the family. At the height of his fame he visited the little church in Carlisle where his grandfather preached. He never forgot that his ancestors had signed the Covenant in Scotland and saw to it that the constitution of the League of Nations bore the same name. His family had settled in the North but in 1855 his father and mother moved from Ohio to Staunton, Virginia, and in the Presbyterian manse there he was born the following year. This accident of birth made him a Southerner who grew up to believe that "all good people were Presbyterians and all bad ones were Yankees." The family escaped most of the hardships of the South in the Civil War, though Wilson as a boy of nine saw Jefferson Davis, President of the Southern Confederacy, being taken off to prison, and was brought up in Columbia, South Carolina, during the ruin and bitterness of reconstruction. Fifty years later when his secretary urged him to take a firmer stand against Mexico after the Villa raid he replied, "The thing that daunts me and holds me back is the aftermath of war with all its tears and tragedies. I come from the South and I know what war is, for I have seen its wreckage and terrible ruin . . . I will not resort to war against Mexico until I have exhausted every measure of keeping out of the mess." Such was the spirit that also prompted his famous "too proud to fight" speech.

As the little boy was delicate he did not receive any formal schooling until he was eleven, and was taught in his early years by his father, whom he admired and respected enormously. The father was a famous pulpit orator and instilled into the son a love of clear and well-ordered prose and a fondness for public speaking that was later to serve him in good stead. At eighteen Wilson entered Princeton, an earnest youth whose hero was Gladstone and whose ambition was to be a great statesman. He did not win distinction as a student but became one of the best speakers of his day, who would only debate in support of subjects in which he believed, and who told his friends, half in jest half in earnest, "Some day I'll argue that point with you in Senate." Then as now, law was the natural avenue to politics but after graduation from the University of Virginia law school, and serving the apprenticeship of waiting for clients that is the lot of most young lawyers, Wilson abandoned it for graduate work in history and political science. He was among the first students at Johns Hopkins, where he met Walter Hines Page, and secured his Ph.D. in 1885 as the author of a book on *Congressional Government,* which foreshadowed his own belief that the President was the natural leader of Congress in legislation. In the next seventeen years the scholar lectured at Bryn Mawr, Wesleyan and Princeton, winning fame as one of the best teachers of government, writing numerous books and articles, but secretly fretting and complaining, "I am so tired of a mere talking profession. I want to do something." His first chance came when he was made President of Princeton in 1902. He vowed to end its days as a "country club". Standards were raised, tutors were engaged and a vain attempt was made to democratize the College by trying to end the social influence of the old clubs. Wilson failed but many of his ideas are now being adopted in Yale and Harvard. Then came a bitter quarrel with the Dean of the Graduate School which ended in defeat when millions were left to expand further the graduate studies. Gladly Wilson found a way out in accepting the Democratic nomination for Governor of New Jersey. He had been chosen by the bosses who realized the strength of the Progressive movement that was sweeping the country but hoped to control this professor in politics. After his election they found they had caught a tartar, as the veteran of many a heated Faculty meeting was well-prepared for the intrigues of bosses. Quickly Wilson sprang into national fame as the progressive leader of a trust-ridden state. His friends, including House, Page and McAdoo, groomed him for the Democratic nomination in 1912 for the Presidency and this he won through the unexpected support of Bryan, whom he had once wished "knocked into a cocked hat." The grudge fight of Taft and Roosevelt had hopelessly split the Republican party; Wilson became the second Democratic president since the Civil War but with less than half of the popular vote.

In keeping with his religious background the new President declared at his inauguration, "This is not a day of triumph but a day for dedication." He shocked old time politicians by his indifference to patronage and later boasted that during his eight years as President he had never invited a Senator or Congressman to lunch or dinner. Though he hungered for affection he had no gift of making himself likeable to the crowd and only sparkled in the company of a few friends. Yet such a man carried through a remarkable program of reform legislation in the first eighteen months of his administration, that evoked from his predecessor

Taft the tribute "I rejoice in the existence of a situation in which the party in power is fulfilling its promises made in the platform and is doing so by following the guidance of the party head who is charged by the people with the party's responsibility." Then came the World War which transformed the domestic reformer into a world figure.

At first Wilson was content to issue a formal proclamation of neutrality and to urge his countrymen to be impartial in thought and feeling, a difficult task for a people of whom over 13,000,000 had been born in European countries. Though Wilson sent his other self, Colonel House, on three missions to Europe that made the Texan more and more pro-Ally, he himself became increasingly suspicious of the good faith of both sides and, when re-nominated in 1916, accepted the party slogan "He kept us out of the War." After his re-election (when he triumphed by a narrow majority in a straight party fight) Wilson told a friend "If we can escape entering the War and bring about a rational peace it is something worth living and dying for and I believe the country feels that way or it would not have re-elected me." A rational peace to him was "a peace without victory", the advocacy of which in January 1917 brought resentment from both sides. Then came the German blunder—a decision to adopt unlimited submarine warfare in defiance of previous pledges to Wilson. Despite his agonized search for an alternative Wilson became convinced that his country must declare war "because there was no other way of defending our rights." True to his moral idealism he urged the country to enter the struggle in the spirit of crusaders "to make the world safe for democracy." It is probable that most of the crusaders felt like the future President Harding who said, "We asked the sons of the republic to defend our national rights rather than purge the old world of its accumulated ills of rivalry and greed." But Wilson as the champion of democracy, self-determination and a League of Nations caught the world's imagination. His typewriter was a weapon of heavy calibre in the fight with Ludendorff. His oratory, never purely emotional since he believed that "eloquence lies in the thought not the throat", moved millions who looked upon him as a new Messiah when the Armistice was signed and his cause seemed to have triumphed.

Then tragedy. At home Wilson exposed himself to the weapons of his opponents by appealing for a Democratic Congress in the mid-term election of 1918. The Republicans rushed to the fray, led by bitter personal enemies of Wilson like Lodge and Roosevelt, captured control of Congress and served notice upon Europe that Woodrow Wilson did not really represent the American people. Ignoring this and against the warnings of his advisers, Wilson decided to attend the Peace Conference in Paris, there to lead the fight for a just peace. As

Churchill has written, when he set sail, "Before him lay the naughty entrenchments of Paris, and behind him, the sullen veto of Senate." When he spoke from Washington it was in Olympian tones, when he entered the arena in Paris it was to debate with men who were far quicker thinkers than himself and who were more used to what Lord Balfour has called "a rough and tumble affair". Never a master of detail, willing to use information but unable to accept advice, Wilson did salvage the League of Nations from the wreckage of his ideals but surrendered on other points. As he remarked, 'I know that I shall be accused of violating my own principles yet nevertheless I must work for world order and organization against anarchy and a return to the old militarism." The weeks of discussion and intrigue in over-heated and unventilated rooms sapped the strength of a man who never was robust, and soured his temper.

Meanwhile, back in Washington, his enemies had their knives sharpened to cut the Treaty and the League to ribbons. Even then they might have been baffled had Wilson been willing to accept a few reservations to the treaty as House, Taft and Lord Grey urged him to do. But the sick man, suspicious of everything and everyone, set his jaw and refused. He would appeal to the people against his enemies on a tour of the country. This tragic trip was interrupted by a complete breakdown in September 1919. Another attack followed in

October and for the rest of his Presidency Wilson was an invalid. The Senate rejected the League, the people rejected the Democratic party in 1920 in what Wilson had hoped would be a solemn referendum on his foreign policy, and the era of Harding and "normalcy" was inaugurated.

Wilson lived three years after his retirement, a noble ruin. He did not live to see Franklin D. Roosevelt, his Assistant Secretary of Navy, who campaigned for the League in 1920, become the next Democratic president of the United States. He did not live to see the League he created fail in its test of collective powers against a law-breaking state while his country adopted neutrality legislation remote from his visions of America's part in a new world order. But the day will come when this man, handicapped as he was by serious defects of temperament, will attain his proper stature in the eyes of the American people. Meanwhile we may apply to him, as his friend and biographer Mrs. Edith Reid has done, Milton's noble lines:

> Servant of God, well done, well has thou fought
> The better fight, who single has maintained
> Against revolted multitudes the Cause of Truth,
> In word mightier than they in Armes:
> And for the testimonie of truth has born
> Universal reproach, far worse to bear
> Than violence; for this was all thy care
> To stand approv'd in sight of God though Worlds
> Judg'd thee perverse.

II

FRANKLIN D. ROOSEVELT AND THE AMERICAN "NEW DEAL"

GROVER Cleveland was the first member of the Democratic Party to become President of the United States after it was shattered by the American Civil War. In 1887 his struggles to give the country an honest and efficient administration had made him highly unpopular with hungry office-seekers, greedy protectionists, bonus-seeking Civil War veterans and currency cranks. His friends boasted "We love him for the enemies he has made." One of these friends from up-state New York called to see him one day and brought along his five-year-old boy. To this boy the harassed President said grimly, "I'll give you a wish to remember for the rest of your life. Pray to God that He never lets you become president of the United States." Despite his mother's frequent reminder of the warning, the boy failed to take it to heart and is now the third Democratic President of the United States since the Civil War. As President, Franklin Delano Roosevelt has become as ardently hated by his own class as Cleveland ever was, but unlike Cleveland he secured, when running for a second term, the largest majority any president has had since the days of James Monroe.

The Roosevelt family can fairly claim to be among the few patrician families of the United States. Its founder arrived in New Amsterdam from Holland in 1650, bringing with him a family Bible which is still among the family's most prized possessions. This pioneer was Claes Martensen, but in the New World he took a new family name, Roosevelt, after his native Dutch village. The Roosevelts prospered as New York prospered but, unlike another Dutch family, the Astors, had a preference for the green fields of the countryside and were pioneers in creating a country home on the banks of the upper Hudson. Here at Hyde Park Franklin Roosevelt was born in 1882. On his maternal side Roosevelt is descended from a Flemish family, the Delanos, likewise long resident in the New World, but possessing a deep-rooted seafaring tradition. Grandfather Delano had captained his own tea clipper to the China coast, so it is not surprising that his grandson had his own little boat in his early 'teens and clamoured to go to sea when it was time to attend private school. The President's holiday sea cruises, his collection of ship models, and his keen interest in the American navy well reflect the Delano tradition.

Franklin Roosevelt had about as happy a childhood as any boy could have. At seven he was riding his own pony, at eleven he had a wide knowledge of wood-lore gained from roaming the woods on the Hudson. Before he was fourteen he had visited Europe with his parents seven times and had already run foul of the German government by being arrested with his tutor four times in a single day for minor infractions of the laws. He was freed from the regular discipline of school life until at 15 he entered Groton, perhaps the most exclusive private school in America. From Groton the young man proceeded naturally to Harvard where he knew the right people, joined the right clubs, and became editor of the college paper, *The Crimson.* Yet there were occasional flashes of independence. Roosevelt once astonished his well-bred friends by supporting the Boers in the South African war and mildly shocked Harvard by editorials in *The Crimson* denouncing the excessive power of the rich in student government.

Almost immediately after graduation at 23 Franklin Roosevelt was married to a distant cousin Elinor, a girl only 20, whose qualities of generosity and eager interest in life were to make her the ablest "first lady of the land" in American history. On their wedding day the bride was given in marriage by her famous kinsman Theodore Roosevelt, President of the United States. Characteristically, "Teddy" monopolized the centre of the stage to the mild discomfiture of the happy couple. After marriage the couple settled in New York, where Mr. Roosevelt studied law at Columbia University and two years later became a partner in a well-known legal firm. But the young lawyer had no pressing need to make his fortune at the bar and had no ambition to become famous as a master of his profession. Like his ancestors before him, he found more happiness at Crum Elbow in the countryside with his family and friends. The latter were shocked when, "encouraged by the glamour of Uncle Ted's example," he decided to emulate the career of his distinguished kinsman and enter New York politics. He was green at the game, as was shown by his appearance at a nominating convention of 1910 dressed in fashionable riding clothes, but he learned quickly. Years later he told how he discovered what the voters wanted. "I went out to tell them what they should have rather than tell them how much of their desire could possibly be secured, and to suggest practical ways to get action. I didn't know what they wanted, but before the end of the campaign I knew what their look meant. . . . They wanted security." And so the young man appeared as a state senator at Albany, a college youngster "still wet behind the ears" according to the Tammany Hall politicians, but shrewd enough to give them a fight when they endeavoured to elect a seasoned war horse as national senator. In Albany he met a newspaperman, Louis McHenry Howe, who was to serve him loyally and effectively on the long road to the White House. The young reformer admired another novice who had entered politics at the same time as himself, Woodrow Wilson, and played his part in securing his hero's nomination for the presidency in 1912. His services were recognized by the offer of an administrative post in Washington and like "T. R." before him, he chose to be Assistant Secretary of the Navy.

Eight years in Washington broadened his circle of acquaintances, gave him invaluable experience of administration and national politics, and deepened his admiration for the president who strove to give America a "New Freedom" and to make the world "safe for democracy". When others, alarmed at Wilson's unpopularity, drew away from him in 1920, Roosevelt remained loyal and at the party convention in that year seized the New York state standard and joined in a demonstration of esteem for their national leader. In the same spirit he accepted the nomination for vice-presidency on the party ticket and preached support of the League of Nations, his chief's great ideal, when it was apparent to most politicians that the Republicans were almost certain to win. They did win, with one of the weakest men who ever entered the White House, Warren Harding, but Franklin Roosevelt had hung up a new record for vigorous campaigning in a good cause. When he left Washington in the spring of 1921 it was with the full intention of enjoying once again the broad acres and pleasant ways of Hyde Park.

Then fate struck a shattering blow. While enjoying a holiday at the family cottage on Campobello Island, off the coast of New Brunswick, Roosevelt was suddenly stricken with infantile paralysis; it left him helpless from the hips down. A weaker man would have bewailed his fate, like Job, and remained an embittered invalid. His doctor said that the will to recover might do wonders in such circumstances and added gloomily "My experience has been that very few people have the courage and determination to make the fight." But Roosevelt was one of the very few. Characteristically he said: "It's ridiculous to tell me that a grown man can't conquer a child's illness." The ever-faithful Howe was to watch silently his chief struggle until the perspiration streamed down his face, in order to move even the smallest foot muscle. His wife helped in the battle for recovery, and from an unknown sympathizer came the suggestion that he try the curative waters of Warm Springs, Georgia. A visit there in 1924 proved greatly beneficial and was the turning-point in the struggle. For the rest of his life Franklin Roosevelt was to wear a steel brace and to walk with the help of others. But he had conquered his disability and remained the master of his fate. Moreover, he had developed a magnificent physique which has enabled him to stand the strain of office far better than any of his immediate predecessors. The famous boxer Gene Tunney once remarked that he had rarely seen a torso, shoulders, neck and wrists so massive and sinewy as those of the President.

It was years before Franklin Roosevelt could play an active part again in politics but he did manage to propose the nomination of his friend Alfred Smith for the presidency in 1924, in a speech of warm friendliness for the "Happy Warrior", as he termed him. Smith was unsuccessful but four years later the Democratic party relented and placed him in nomination against Herbert Hoover. At Smith's earnest appeal Roosevelt reluctantly agreed to take the nomination for governor of New York state in succession to his friend. Smith was defeated but Roosevelt was more fortunate and was installed in January 1939 in the state capital where he had served his apprenticeship. As governor he was popular and successful, winning a second term with a record majority of over 700,000. There was a hint of the "New Deal" in those days when he said in a dispute over power rights, "Public utility corporations must never be our masters. They must be our servants." As New York has been proverbially a stepping-stone to the White

House, James Farley, a born politician, began to tour the country to pave the way for his nomination in 1932, and a group of Columbia professors, headed by Raymond Moley, were eager to assist in drafting new policies and organizing campaign material. At Chicago the Democrats rejected Al Smith's hopes for a second nomination and to his resentment selected his successor at Albany. Breaking all precedents, the nominee flew to Chicago and told the Convention, "I pledge myself to a New Deal for the American people. This is more than a political campaign. It is a call to arms."

It was not hard to beat Herbert Hoover in 1932; the depression had already done so, but it took courage to face the situation in March 1933, when Franklin Roosevelt was inaugurated as thirty-second president of the United States. Banks were popping like fire-crackers, millions were unemployed and embittered at the absence of organized relief, confidence was gone in the business leaders who had seemed all-wise and all-powerful in the boom days. To a discouraged nation came a reminder from the new president, "the only thing we have to fear is fear itself," an indictment of unscrupulous "money-changers", and a promise of leadership "dedicated to a disciplined attack upon our common problems." "For the trust imposed in me," said the new president, "I will return the courage and devotion that befit the time. I can do no other."

With this pledge of action the "New Deal" was inaugurated to take up the task of reform where its forerunners, the "New Nationalism" of Theodore Roosevelt and the "New Freedom" of Woodrow Wilson, had left off. The President brought to his post as great gifts of showmanship as the other President Roosevelt, but greater courage and a keener appreciation of the problems which confronted the nation. When H. G. Wells visited the Roosevelts in 1934 he felt as he talked with his hosts "here in the White House an unblinkered mind in possession." That quality of open mindedness and experimentation, lacking in Woodrow Wilson, has impressed every student of this period. Sometimes the experimentation has succeeded, at other times it has been ill-conceived and badly executed. But never has the attempt been abandoned. As Mr. Roosevelt told a college audience in 1938, "Democratic methods within a nation's life entail change—the kind of change through local processes described by Mr. Justice Cardozo—the kind of changes to meet new social and economic needs through recognized processes of government." Such changes must come in this rapidly evolving world of ours and it is to the credit of the President and to the discredit of those he christened the "economic royalists", that progress has been made. At the hands of their President the American people are receiving an education, and a costly one, which causes as independent a critic as Charles Beard to declare that "President Roosevelt has made a more profound impression upon the political, social and economic thought of America than any or all of his predecessors." When he leaves the White House there may, and probably will be, some departures from the policies and institutions he has created, but there can be neither retreat nor destruction.

What democratic peoples outside the United States, including ourselves, are now most concerned about is the success or failure of the President in educating the American people to their international responsibilities. In his policy of liberal trade agreements, for which his Secretary of State, Mr. Cordell Hull, must also receive considerable praise, he made a bold attack upon the log-jam that had reduced international trade to a mere trickle. In his "Good Neighbour Policy" he created a harmony in this western hemisphere that was in pleasing contrast to the struggles of fear-ridden Europe. In his efforts to make the American people realize that they with the other democracies face a common danger, the President is treading upon the hazardous ground which gave way beneath the stubborn tread of Woodrow

Wilson twenty years ago. Many Americans believe, as President Roosevelt told Congress in January 1939, "The defence of religion, democracy and good faith among nations is all the same fight," but more take comfort from the President's reassurance in his broadcast on the day Britain entered the war, that "as long as it remains within my power to prevent it, there will be no blackout of peace in the United States." Yet President Roosevelt, in contrast to his former chief Woodrow Wilson, did not urge the American people to be impartial in thought as well as action, but remarked significantly, "Even a neutral cannot be asked to close his mind or his conscience."

The latest move, to repeal the mandatory clause of the Neutrality Act imposing an embargo on shipments of arms to belligerents, was described by the chief executive as a move to keep America out of the war, but was also of material aid to the Allies in making available the resources of American munition plants and aeroplane factories, under the cash-and-carry clause. How much further President Roosevelt may lead his people towards co-operation with the European democracies in the struggle against Hitlerism, is among the imponderables of the tragic future.

III

MARSHAL HINDENBURG AND THE GERMAN REPUBLIC

HAD Paul von Beneckendorff and Hindenburg, Field Marshal and twice President of Germany, died in 1913, he would have been dismissed by a few lines in the German press for he was one who had greatness thrust upon him at an age when his life work seemed over.

At the present time his reputation is undergoing critical scrutiny. Ten years ago a German liberal scholar, Dr. Jäckh, now in exile, praised Hindenburg as the George Washington of his country, "first in war, first in peace, and first in the hearts of his countrymen." To him the president was a striking example of education in democracy by responsibility, and his historic mission was to win over the German middle class to support of the republic. But in 1932 a young Englishman, Mr. J. W. Wheeler Bennett, was amazed at being told by a distinguished naval officer: "Hindenburg's record is a bad one—Ludendorff won his battles and he betrayed Ludendorff; the Kaiser made him Field-Marshal and he betrayed the Kaiser; the Right elected him in 1925 and he betrayed the Right;

the Left elected him in 1932 and he has betrayed the Left." Such a savage verdict astounded the Englishman, who set himself to examine its accuracy. His investigations are embodied in a recent life of Hindenburg which bears the subtitle "The Wooden Titan", a most able and enlightening study, to which this author is indebted. "The old General was," he says, "a figure-head carved upon the brow of the German barque to ward off evil spirits and to bring good fortune . . . The German people had created for themselves an idol, not of clay but of wood, which the dry rot of intrigue would enter and destroy leaving but a hollow shell." Let us examine the basis for this verdict.

Paul von Beneckendorff and Hindenburg (it was not until 1914 that he chose to be known simply as Hindenburg) was born in the Province of Posen, East Germany, in 1847, the son of a retired army officer whose family had been country squires and soldiers for generations. The estate was steeped in the tradition of service to the Hohenzollerns. Writing of his boyhood the old General describes his talks with a gardener who had fought with Frederic the Great, and comments "There fell across my childhood a beam from the glorious Frederician past." At eleven he entered the Prussian Cadet Corps to serve his king like his ancestors before him and to follow in the well-worn path of duty and service to the state. At eighteen he fought with his regiment against the Austrians, winning a decoration for bravery and being wounded. Four years later he marched to Paris with the triumphal German army and again was decorated for his courage. Then followed forty years of quiet and unpretentious service in the army in which he climbed steadily up the ladder of promotion. Everybody liked and respected the towering giant of transparent simplicity of character but none saw in him a military genius. When, after forty-five years of service, he left the army, it was not even thought advisable to keep Hindenburg on the special reserve in the event of war. His one thought was of peace and quiet and of hope that his son, also in the army, would carry on the family tradition of loyal service.

The World War gave Hindenburg an undreamed of opportunity. He promptly offered his services but was at first passed over, so that he complained to an old friend, "I am ashamed to show my face in the streets." Then came a telegram ordering him to prepare for service in East Prussia and to meet on the train at Hanover his future colleague, a much younger general, Eric Ludendorff, who had already won fame by capturing Liége. The two generals were being sent to command the army defending East Prussia against the Russians, since the German commander had suffered a loss of nerve. It was in Ludendorff that General Moltke, the chief of staff, said he placed unbounded confidence. But Ludendorff was known as a highly-strung man and a partner of more phlegmatic temperament would be a useful foil. Someone thought of Hindenburg as the perfect type for such a part and gave him his chance. Ludendorff had already mapped out a plan of campaign with which the retired officer concurred. So was well established the close partnership of what Foch called the general and the patriot.

By August 29th the Russians had been crushingly defeated, their general a suicide, three army corps destroyed, and 200,000 men killed or taken prisoner. The authors of the brilliant victory were Ludendorff and General Hoffmann although Hindenburg did support his chief of staff by his steadiness of nerve when a series of alarming reports tempted him to modify his plans. But the German people knew nothing of the tactics and were only too eager to idolize a hero in the East especially as it became clear that none would appear in the West. The Hindenburg legend had been created and, in the shadow of the hero, Ludendorff manoeuvred for more power. Moltke's successor saw the danger and vainly attempted to separate HL, as Churchill calls them, but by August 1916 the partners were in supreme command, establishing a virtual dictatorship which neither the Kaiser nor the Chancellor dared defy. More and more

Hindenburg became merely the symbol; towards the close of the war, as Colonel Bauer has testified, "we did not even tell him where the army corps were stationed."

When Ludendorff's nerves gave way after the black day of Amiens in August 1918 he roused the 70-year-old general from his grandiose dreams to force him to demand from the Emperor the opening of peace negotiations. On October 2nd they told the new Chancellor that "the bad news from the Balkans and the lack of reserves made victory impossible. It was imperative to stop fighting in order to spare further useless sacrifices and the loss of thousands of brave soldiers' lives." This statement is the best reply to the present German fable that the army was stabbed in the back by the Jews, sailors and Socialists who caused Germany's defeat. It shocked the government but they could do nothing but open negotiations for peace. When Wilson's harsh terms were known, Ludendorff returned to a fight-to-a-finish policy but it was too late. When the two generals urged the army to follow that course the Chancellor forced Ludendorff's resignation. Hindenburg was equally culpable but let his colleague in insubordination go alone. He remained at G. H. Q. and there faced the painful task of telling the Emperor, who had come there from Berlin, that the army would no longer support him. Here again he placed a part of the responsibility upon his new colleague, General Gröner. When the Emperor had fled, the Field Marshal had to decide where his duty lay. With the loyalty that was his finest quality Hindenburg decided to stay with his men and lead them home. In so doing he probably saved Germany from Bolshevism but likewise stopped the revolution before it had gone far enough for the future safety of the republic. The Kaiser had gone, but the generals remained and there was no Cromwell, Carnot or Trotsky to create a new people's army. It was to Hindenburg that the government of the republic turned for advice when they read the harsh terms of the peace treaties, repugnant to every German. Much against his will Hindenburg realized that to resume battle was impossible. But to Gröner he said, "There is no need for me to stay, you can tell the President as well as I." Gröner loyally carried out the commission and for fourteen years when fiercely attacked as a traitor by extreme nationalists, kept silent as to Hindenburg's responsibility for the advice. As he told a friend, "It was necessary that one great German figure should emerge from the war free from all blame that was attached to the German general staff. That figure had to be Hindenburg."

After the army was demobilized Hindenburg retired again to Hanover where, with the help of a ghost writer, he wrote his memoirs and convinced himself that Germany had never been beaten on the battlefield. In 1925 the Socialist president of the Republic died suddenly and the conservative parties of the Right endeavoured to secure control of the Presidency. When, on the first ballot, no candidate secured a clear majority they determined to draft Hindenburg into service. The old veteran grumbled but the skilful plea of duty to the state voiced by Admiral Tirpitz won him over, and millions of Germans supported him on a platform of "Join with me in helping to secure the re-establishment of the Fatherland."

For five years the "old gentleman", as he was affectionately called, worked loyally with his various Chancellors from Stresemann, the business man and good European, to Müller the trades unionist and Socialist. His eightieth birthday was the occasion for a demonstration of affection, and was also marked by the gift to him of a large property in East Prussia which had once belonged to his family. The Socialist President of the Reichstag voiced the nation's feelings when he said "from the day of his accession to office he has acted as the representative of his whole nation and not as the spokesman of a party, and he has always raised his voice on behalf of conciliation and compromise." One wonders if in a concentration camp six years later Herr Löbe would have repeated those remarks.

When the hurricane of the depression swept over Germany, President Hindenburg was caught unprepared like most of us. A stronger Chancellor was found, Heinrich Brüning, now a professor at Harvard, and emergency decrees were used to strengthen the state in a fashion undreamed of when the constitution was drafted. But Brüning had to face the unpopularity of every statesman in depression times and Hitler, who seemed doomed to obscurity in 1928, increased his party in the Reichstag from 12 to 107 in 1930. The Nationalists who had been disappointed in Hindenburg as "their man" turned to watch this new and menacing factor. When the time drew round for presidential elections Hitler refused to consider any extension of the old soldier's term. With a heavy heart Hindenburg agreed to stand again, this time as the bulwark of the republic with the backing of the Catholic and Socialist parties, while the Right savagely attacked him as the man who had destroyed the very thing he had fought for as Field Marshal. However the Field Marshal could still, in spite of the depression, command more respect than the corporal Hitler and emerged triumphant with a majority over Hitler of over six million. But as Hitler boasted, "He is 85, I am 43; I can afford to wait."

To many abroad and in Germany it seemed as though the worst was over. In 1931 Brüning had obtained a moratorium on reparations; in

1932 he was within an ace of securing equality in armaments. Then came the incredible news of his dismissal by the President who had publicly praised him as the best chancellor since Bismarck. Why had Brüning been knifed? The reason seems to have been that the Junker class to which Hindenburg belonged were fearful of his proposal to break up the hopelessly insolvent large estates which the government had subsidized, and had worked on the old man when on his estate to stop this danger of "agrarian bolshevism". Cut to the heart by his treatment Brüning retired and the way was cleared for Hitler.

Meanwhile palace intriguers had found a gentleman, whom Hindenburg liked, to become Chancellor, Franz von Papen, an almost unknown figure except in the Junker and moneyed circles. To him Hindenburg gave two elections in order to secure a majority in Parliament, but with no success. Then it was Von Papen's turn to retire, though Hindenburg let him go with regret. Another schemer assumed office, General Von Schleicher. Von Papen, embittered at his dismissal, intrigued with Hitler, whom the old President had flatly refused to consider as Chancellor in August 1932. It was agreed that Hindenburg should be prevailed upon to accept Hitler as Chancellor, with Von Papen as Vice-Chancellor and a majority of experts and nationalists holding Cabinet posts. Once again the palace clique worked upon the old man with their cries of dangers of agrarian bolshevism, and Von Schleicher went the way of his predecessors. On January 30, 1933, Hitler was sworn in as Chancellor and the future Marshal Göring said piously, "How gloriously had the aged Field Marshal been used as an instrument in the hand of God." That evening, so the story goes, Hitler and Hindenburg reviewed together a torchlight procession of Nazi storm troopers and nationalist Steel Helmets, a symbol of the union of nationalist and Nazi. The Brown Shirts went past first in sloppy formation; the Steel Helmets, all war veterans, marched with military precision. An observer was said to have heard Hindenburg, his mind wandering, remark: "Ludendorff, how well your men are marching and what a lot of prisoners they have taken!"

Hindenburg lived eighteen months longer to see his friends insulted, his church menaced, and his former colleagues dead, in prison, or in exile. He immured himself on his estate, a giant ghost of the past. The terrible blood purge of June 30, 1934, which struck down so many of all parties and classes, only drew from him a telegram, which many believe to have been sent without his consent, of "profound thanks and sincere appreciation". The huge frame had at last weakened and he slowly sank to his grave. When his doctor told him on August 1, 1934, that "Friend Hein", the

German nickname for Death, was walking round the house, he asked to confer with the Lord a little and then said, "It's all right now, Sauerbruch, now tell Friend Hein he can come in."

The next day the old Field Marshal was dead and the last personal obstacle to full power for the Austrian corporal had been removed. The Wooden Titan had fallen at last.

IV

GUSTAV STRESEMANN, GERMAN PATRIOT AND GOOD EUROPEAN

OF the men whose achievements we are surveying, Gustav Stresemann underwent the greatest transformation and experienced the cruellest fate. The nationalist who clamoured for the retention of Belgium by Germany because "every foot of her soil had been hallowed by German blood", who looked, as an eyewitness related, as if he had been pole-axed when a staff officer told a group of party leaders in October 1918 that Germany was beaten, who telegraphed on behalf of his party loyal greetings to the Kaiser in 1919 and visited the Crown Prince in exile, two years later became the sincere Republican who ordered the Ambassadors abroad to celebrate the anniversary of the founding of the Republic, the democratic statesman whose last plans were for the creation of a new party to fight the forces of reaction that threatened the state, and the good European who was awarded the Nobel Peace prize in 1926. Wilson failed to get the United States to follow his lead in becoming a partner in the struggle for world peace but he will never be forgotten in

Geneva and is loyally defended by his friends at home. Stresemann failed to secure the full measure of co-operation that he expected from his English and French colleagues and today the Nazis are determined that the sponge of oblivion shall erase his name from the German tablets. The street which bore his name in Berlin was renamed. The monument erected on the Rhine in gratitude for the departure of the French troops five years ahead of schedule was torn down. The policy of fulfilment gave way to the policy of bullying and sword rattling which eventually produced "encirclement" of Germany and another world war. All that he stood for at home is in ruin. The greatest German Foreign Secretary since Bismarck lies in his grave unwept, unhonoured and unsung.[1]

Gustav Stresemann was born in Berlin in May 1878, of a middle class family of moderate means, his father being a brewer's agent. As a boy he grew up in the atmosphere of heady nationalism and exuberant self-confidence that characterized the German Empire under Bismarck. His scholastic ability encouraged his family to send him to University and first at Berlin and later in the University of Leipzig he pursued his studies in philosophy, political science, and economics until he secured his Ph.D. In his college days he was regarded as somewhat of a romantic idealist,

[1] The latest edition of his biography by his private secretary is entitled *Frustration, or Stresemann's Race with Death.*

steeped in the poetry of Uhland and Lenau, writing verse himself and worshipping, as he did all his life, at the shrines of Goethe and Napoleon. In the student corps to which he belonged and of which he was the chief orator he was christened "Bertrand De Born", after the romantic hero of Uhland's ballad. The student may have had his head in the clouds but he kept his feet firmly planted on the ground; for business reasons he wrote his Ph.D. thesis on the prosaic subject, "The German Beer Bottling Industry". On graduation he accepted a post as secretary of the Saxon chocolate manufacturer's union and showed such marked organizing ability that at 25 he was the secretary of the Union of Saxon Manufacturers, increasing its membership in two years from 180 to 1000. His first experience in politics came as a member of the Dresden town council, and shortly after, in 1907, he was elected to the German Reichstag as a member of the National Liberal party, with the reputation in Socialist circles of being "a stiff-necked, pushing, relentless employer union-executive". In the party he was somewhat unpopular but respected for his forcefulness; he was hailed laughingly by the leader as its Crown Prince in 1912.

When war broke out Stresemann like millions of others saw it as a crusade to defend Germany against a host of jealous neighbours, and gave the Supreme Command his fullest support. A weak heart kept him from military service but he followed with ardour the progress of the war and kept a picture of Ludendorff in his study. He was one of the keenest critics of the feeble leadership of Chancellor Bethmann-Hollweg and helped to overthrow him in 1917. He was then looked upon as an important political figure, having been chosen leader of the National Liberals in 1916. Stresemann was bitterly disappointed that he was not invited to join the cabinet of Prince Max of Baden in October 1918, when the latter was asked to form a Cabinet to bridge the gap between autocratic and constitutional government. Though a Nationalist statesman he had never been a blind reactionary and supported a broadening of the franchise and democratic government, arguing up to the Revolution that "we are and remain Monarchists . . . and are convinced that by energetic co-operation to realize the new order we are at the same time doing the best possible thing to preserve the Monarchy." When the Revolution came in November it seemed that Stresemann's political career was at an end. He was distrusted by the new government, his party had disappeared and the larger section of it which helped to form the new Democratic party was not prepared to admit him to its ranks. Undaunted, Stresemann built up a new group known as "the People's party", which was subsidized by Big Business and retained its preference for Monarchy. Such a party could elect only 23 members in a house of over 400. It voted against acceptance of the Treaty of Versailles and seemed likely to hold aloof permanently from the new régime.

The great change in Stresemann's views came late in 1922. In a chance conversation with one of the high officials of the war period he discovered, in the latter's scornful disclosures, that he and his colleagues, who had backed the unrestricted submarine campaign so warmly, had been deliberately cheated by its advocates who knew as Helfferich told him: "It could not succeed. We had very few U-boats when we began the U-boat war, the Admiralty always refused to build them. And later when we declared unlimited U-boat warfare, we had utterly miscalculated our powers of construction." The revelation of such cynical duplicity and incompetence horrified Stresemann and drove him to support the Republic which might check the repetition of such a system. As his biographer said, "He had entered upon the road to Damascus." Soon after in a speech in Parliament he foreshadowed his future policy by pleading for economic co-operation between France and Germany, by reminding his countrymen that Poincaré did not represent all French opinion and by urging the Foreign Minister to "grasp the earliest opportunity of getting in touch with France."

Stresemann's first chance to show his powers as a statesman came in August 1923 at one of the darkest moments in German history. Since January France had been in occupation of the Ruhr Valley, the industrial heart of Germany, in an attempt to collect reparations payment of which Poincaré was convinced his country had been defrauded. Germany had followed a policy of passive resistance, subsidizing the miners of the Ruhr to remain idle. That policy made the occupation almost sterile but also destroyed completely the value of the German mark. The cabinet resigned in despair and Stresemann took the thankless post of Chancellor. His son asked him if he knew what he was in for but with his usual courageous optimism the father answered, "If I did not realize it I should not feel so cheerful. I was not meant to hold a sinecure. But don't you worry: all will yet be well."

His first step was to make overtures to Poincaré to see what France would offer in return for the abandonment of passive resistance. No concession came from the implacable Lorrainer and Stresemann, knowing that further resistance was useless, called off the campaign unconditionally. This action made him the best hated man in Germany and made his administration a short-lived one but it paved the way for the creation of the Dawes committee to examine the Reparations problem, and ended a fatal deadlock. Before his resignation in November he had also shown his courage by suppressing a Communist revolt in Saxony and a Nazi rising in Munich, the famous "beer-cellar putsch" which seemed at that time to have ended the career of Adolf Hitler. As Hitler never forgives or forgets, Stresemann's part in this episode may well account for the dislike of his predecessor.

When Stresemann resigned as Chancellor his successor induced him to remain in the Cabinet as Foreign Secretary, a post which he was to hold in the numerous coalition Cabinets of that period, until his death. His position made him a key figure in the London negotiations before the Dawes Plan came into operation in 1924 and gave him his first contact with British and French statesmen. He returned from London convinced that Germany would gain far more by a policy of fulfilling to the limit of her capacity her obligations under the Peace Treaty than by a policy of equivocation and delay which only bred distrust abroad and gave men like Poincaré their chance. Such a policy of fulfillment would lead, he was convinced, to a modification of the more draconic sections of the Treaty of Versailles. The advocacy of such views by a man who had formerly been so ardent a Nationalist, made them all the more impressive in Germany but drew upon him the hatred of his former associates and made him, as Lord D'Abernon, the British Ambassador in Berlin and close friend of Stresemann, said, "a poor insurance risk for the rest of his life." Indeed, when he left to conclude the Locarno agreements it was necessary to keep secret the time and place of his departure.

The outward and visible sign of this new policy was the offer of a security pact to France early in 1925 in which Germany recognized as permanent her western frontier and agreed to sign an "all-in" arbitration treaty with France and Belgium and not to change her eastern frontier by force. The guarantee of security in the West was to be strengthened by an Anglo-Italian promise to come to the help of the injured party if either France or Germany broke the pact. It took nine months of difficult negotiations to work out the details of this offer, (which was an amplification of earlier suggestions), during which time Stresemann had to gain English confidence, allay French suspicion and avert German discontent. But he succeeded and in December 1925 the agreements were formally signed in London. There Stresemann in a fine speech declared "Each one of us must first be a citizen of his own country, a good Englishman, a good Frenchman, a good German, a member of his own nation, but each also a citizen of Europe linked together by the great conception of civilization which imbues our continent. We have a right to speak of a European idea . . . If we go down we go down together, if we wish to scale the heights, we cannot do so in conflict with each other but only by a community of effort. In this common effort must be sought the foundation of the future." The sky seemed to have cleared at last and Sir Austen Chamberlain spoke of Locarno as the dividing line between war and peace.

The following year Stresemann made his appearance at Geneva, as Locarno was conditional upon German entry into the League of Nations as a Great Power with a permanent seat on the Council. Then he became both popular and respected. He and Briand cemented their friendship and in their famous luncheon at Thoiry discussed ambitious schemes for the return of the Saar, the evacuation of the Rhineland and the commercialization of the reparation payments. But it was not to be. Wall Street was too engrossed in the American boom to assist in marketing the securities. Paris was again under the sway of Poincaré, who had returned to office to save the franc, and who for the next two years kept Briand in close rein. Stresemann waited hopefully for generous concessions to the new Germany which he personified but nothing of importance came. He was to say to Briand sadly in 1928, "We have lost two precious years." When he arrived in Paris in August of that year to sign the Pact of Paris, the first German Foreign Secretary to visit there since Bismarck, he was warmly greeted by his friend, but Briand saw with dismay a broken man whom overwork, worry and disappointment had placed within sight of the grave at the early age of 50.

Against his doctor's orders he took part in the protracted negotiations that brought in yet another reparations policy, the Young Plan, which did give Germany the promise of evacuation of the Rhineland by July 1, 1930. That was Stresemann's last victory in diplomacy. When he addressed the League Assembly in September 1929 the audience saw a man whose clothes hung loosely around his shrunken form, whose eyes had lost their sparkle, whose breath came in hurried gasps and whose hands clutched the balustrade for support. Says his biographer, "The embodiment of death stood yonder on the tribune and the assemblage bowed involuntarily before its dreadful majesty." Back in Germany he laboured to keep the government together, feeling as he said, "I am truly Germany's last defence against Fascist chaos . . . As long as I am here I cannot leave my post." On October 2 he saved the government by a brilliant speech and came home exhausted. "Well, I've managed it but it was hard—very hard." The next morning he was found dead in his room. With him perished the spirit of Locarno.

V

ADOLF HITLER, "DER FUHRER" OF GERMANY

ON Armistice Day, 1918, a young German corporal was lying in hospital in a quiet Pomeranian town, almost blinded from the effects of a British gas shell that had wounded him near Ypres. When the chaplain brought the news he burst into tears for the first time since the death of his mother, tears of grief that the struggles and sacrifices of his comrades and himself had all been in vain. His future was gloomy. Here he was a man with almost no friends, with no advantage of birth, education or physique, with no qualifications for any profession or skilled trade, living as a voluntary exile from his own country in a land passing under the control of men—the Social Democrats—who he felt had stabbed the German army in the back. Today that young corporal, just past fifty, is Commander-in-Chief of the German army, Chancellor and President of Germany for life, Der Führer, or Leader of the German People, Aggrandizer of the Reich.[1] Adolf Hitler, the Austrian, wields more

[1] The last title was conferred upon him after the annexations of the spring of 1939.

International News Photo

ADOLF HITLER AND VON HINDENBURG

power in Germany than ever did either Bismarck the Iron Chancellor or Kaiser Wilhelm II. In him Austria has avenged her defeat by Bismarck in 1866. Upon his shoulders rests the odium of having plunged Europe again into War. Who and what manner of man is this who has climbed to such dizzy heights of power?

Adolf Hitler was born in 1889 at Braunau, a frontier town of Upper Austria. His father was a petty customs official of obscure origin, his mother a sickly unhappy woman, the third wife of a man twenty-three years her senior. While he was still a boy his father retired on pension and was bitterly disappointed that his son showed no inclination to train himself to follow his father's career. On the contrary, he talked of being an artist and deliberately wasted his time in school except in a few classes like history, geography and drawing. Schoolmates who jeered at his weakness for atlases were told scornfully "I am wiping out the German boundaries, making them larger"—a significant clue to the tenor of his dreams. His teacher was a Pan-German, who deepened the already strong sense of German nationalism that had made him, as a child, wonder why Austria did not fight beside the other German states in the Franco-Prussian War. Hitler grew up with a contempt for the Hapsburg rulers of Austria-Hungary who lacked a sense of German patriotism and were ever ready to preserve their power by playing off one racial group against the other. Years later he wrote of the Sarajevo assassination: "It was the fist of the goddess of Eternal right and pitiless retribution that struck down the deadliest enemy of Austrian Germanism, the Archduke Franz Ferdinand." The father died in 1903, the mother five years later, and, at 19, the adventurer set off to make himself "somebody" in Vienna, "with only a suitcase with clothes and linen in my hand but with an invincible determination in my heart."

Vienna was unkind to him. The Academy of Art refused to accept him as a student though it suggested he might study architecture. But he had little money and that was out of the question. For "five years of misery and desolation", as his autobiography describes them, Hitler struggled for a living, at times sleeping in the humblest lodging houses, peddling his own postcards and getting odd jobs as a builder's helper or house-painter. He might have had a more secure position had he joined a trades union as his mates in the building trade wanted him to do, but pride in his middle class origin prevented. Thus he tells us how at the lunch hour "I sat aside drinking my bottle of milk and eating my piece of bread and carefully studied my new surroundings and contemplated my unhappy life." These years of adversity gave him a genuine sympathy with the poor and unfortunate and also a trace of bitterness at the good fortune of those with wealth and education, who he once complained could show diplomas when he could not. These years also enforced a simple way of living that has survived. Unlike General Göring, Hitler has no taste for flashy uniforms; he is almost an ascetic in matters of diet, and his favorite recreations are listening to music, especially that of Wagner, and walking in the Bavarian hills, where he has his favourite home. This simplicity and indifference to worldly things has had a great appeal to the idealistic youth of Germany and has won for him a personal affection which no other Nazi leader seems to have gained.

In Vienna Hitler was confirmed in his Pan-German convictions and acquired his anti-Jewish beliefs that have caused such misery in Germany. As the capital of an empire of 50,000,000 people of a dozen nations Vienna was a cosmopolitan city where German, Czech, Pole, Croat and Italian rubbed shoulders; a city where the Jew, since the time of the Rothschilds, was prominent in finance and aggressive in the professions and arts. For the first time in his life Hitler heard a babel of tongues and saw the clash of nationalities in which the German often got the worst of it. For the first time he saw the Orthodox Jew with his long caftan and black side-curls, a sight that repelled him and made him an easy convert to the anti-Jewish teachings of the Burgomaster of Vienna. In disgust Hitler left Vienna for Munich in 1913, an embryo fanatic who was, in his own words, "a convinced anti-Semite, a mortal enemy of the Marxian philosophy and a Pan-German." This pathological hatred of the Jew appears in its crudest form in his autobiography and inspires such statements as "So today I believe that I act according to the mind of the Almighty Creator. In beating off the Jew I fight for the work of the Lord." Vienna was not to see him again until his triumphal entry in March, 1938.

In Munich, Hitler was made happier but still had no success at the business of living. When the War came he would not return to Austria to fight for a dynasty he despised, and asked permission to enlist in a Bavarian regiment. This was granted and with a light heart the volunteer set off for the Western front. There he served for the period of the war, receiving the Iron Cross for gallantry, being wounded twice, reaching the rank of corporal, and doing his duty manfully as a cog in the war machine directed by Hindenburg and Ludendorff. In the army he was still a friendless man who cared nothing for leave, wrote no letters, and received no parcels.

Corporal Hitler was not demobilized directly after his return from hospital but was used as a political agent among the troops to preserve their morale against the influence of revolutionary propaganda, of which the officers were keenly suspicious, and to report on the aims and tactics of the numerous new parties. His duties brought him in contact with a German Workers' party founded by a locksmith, Anton Drexler. Although he already dreamed of founding his own party, Hitler accepted an invitation to join the inner group who controlled this struggling movement, and became the seventh member in July 1919, "the most decisive event of my life." In September Hitler made his first speech, which was, characteristically, a diatribe against the Treaty of Versailles, and discovered his gifts as an orator. Soon after he helped to draft the 25 points of the party platform in conjunction with Drexler and Gottfield Feder, the latter an engineer with radical ideas about the thraldom of interest that appealed to him. The platform reflects his pre-war views, with almost one-fifth of it attacking the Jews, "who cannot be regarded as fellow countrymen," and another section demanding "the union of all Germans in a Pan-German state, the abrogation of the Treaty of Versailles and Saint-Germain and equal rights with all other nations." The radical section of the manifesto, which explains the party's claim to be a National-Socialist movement, demanded the abolition of unearned incomes, the nationalization of all trusts, the break-up of departmental stores, the reform of the system of land-holding, the confiscation of war profits and various measures of social reform. Most of the policies were designed to appeal to the middle class, sinking in the economic scale but unwilling to associate with an international Marxian movement. Hitler became chairman of the propaganda section of the party and took for his model the British war-time efforts, which greatly impressed him by their directness and simplicity. He decided that to influence large masses of people it was necessary "to concentrate on a few essential points, never to allow them to be lost sight of, to enunciate the principles in the form of a categorical statement, to exercise the greatest possible patience in disseminating ideas, and to be infinitely patient in awaiting results." He despised mob mentality: "The German has no idea how much the people must be misled if the support of the masses is required."

The people of Munich were given plenty of opportunities to hear, as Bruce Lockhart did in 1922, this "little black-haired man in riding boots and a cheap brown waterproof, haranguing a mixed crowd of 200 men and women from a soapbox in short jerky sentences." Men as varied in experience as General Ludendorff, Captain Röhm, the ex-aviator Göring, and the Baltic exile, Dr. Rosenberg, were co-operating with the orator whom Munich called the "drummer" because of his success in getting recruits. Germany was startled by Hitler's attempt on the 9th of November, 1923, to march on "that sinful Babylon, Berlin," and rule a state shaken to its foundations by the French occupation of the Ruhr. Even though he had the co-operation of General Ludendorff,, the Bavarians were not prepared to follow his banner, and the professional troops of the Reichswehr easily disposed, in a few volleys, of what was scornfully called the "Beer-cellar Putsch". Hitler and Ludendorff were tried for treason. His great services in the past secured acquittal for Ludendorff but Hitler received a sentence of five years' imprisonment. A too lenient government set him free after six months in prison, a period which was used for writing most of his 780-page autobiography, *Mein Kampf* ("My Struggle"). The book is turgid and long-winded, incoherent and bombastic. It is also frightening in its fanaticism and harsh in its avowals of a foreign policy that will give a German people, who must number 250,000,000 by the end of the century, living space (*Lebensraum*). In Germany, over five million copies have been sold and the book remains the Bible of National Socialism. What Hitler the revolutionary dreamed in prison has become a political programme, to which the Soviet-German Pact is a striking exception.[1]

[1] For a brief incisive analysis of *Mein Kampf*, see R. C. K. Ensor, *Herr Hitler's Self-Disclosure in Mein Kampf*, Oxford Pamphlets on World Affairs, No. 3.

Freed from prison Hitler set to work to reorganize his shattered party, but progress was slow. At the end of 1926 there were less than 50,000 members. Economic conditions were improving with the working of the Dawes Plan and, in the elections of 1928, the party sent only 12 deputies to a Reichstag of 490. So shrewd an observer as Lord D'Abernon, the British ambassador, could write in his diary that after his release from prison Hitler "faded into oblivion." Yet the young people, the disinherited and the dispossessed, were becoming more and more restless and in 1929 Stresemann, the Foreign Secretary, said bitterly to an English friend, ". . . but can they not see that the ground is slipping away under my feet? The youth of Germany, which we might have won for peace and the new Europe, we both have lost. That is my tragedy and your crime."

Then came the Great Depression, the dizzy rise of the figures of unemployment and the further disillusionment of the middle classes. Hitler gave them circuses in his colourful meetings and promised them bread. The result was seen in the elections of 1930, when the number of Nazi deputies jumped from 12 to 107. This group, whose average age was 28, faced triumphantly in the Reichstag the disheartened Social Democrats, whose average age was 45. The depression deepened, Brüning's efforts seemed useless and unemployment reached over six millions in the winter of 1932. When Hindenburg stood for re-election as President, Hitler dared oppose him. He was beaten but thirteen millions had voted for him, twice as many as in 1930. Six weeks later the old President abruptly dismissed Chancellor Brüning and an intrigue made Von Papen Chancellor. The latter was given an election to see if he could rally support for a government of the pre-war type—the Monocle Cabinet, as it was called. The elections of July gave the Nazis 230 members, the largest group in the Reichstag. Twice the old general interviewed the ex-corporal to see if he would enter a coalition with Von Papen. Twice he refused, demanding all or nothing. Another election in November brought Von Papen no nearer control of Parliament, though it did reduce the Nazi strength to 195 and raised the Communists to their peak figure of 100. In desperation, the President summoned, on December 4, General Von Schleicher who formed a government pledged "to find work and avoid political experiments." The Nazi cause seemed doomed and on that day an English observer saw in Berlin "dejected-looking young men in brown shirts, rattling money-boxes timidly and without response in the faces of unheeding passers-by." Then more intrigue. Von Papen and Hitler met secretly in Cologne. Big Business, fearful of Communism, was reassured about Nazi policies. Hitler was ready now to accept a coalition if he could be Chancellor. Hindenburg was reached by secret influences and, like Brüning, Von Schleicher was wounded in the house of his friends. He resigned and, on January 30, 1933, Hitler became Chancellor.

Thirteen years of propaganda and six weeks of intrigue had done their work. Today Adolf Hitler is the head of a totalitarian state in which all open opposition has disappeared. Like Mussolini, he has trampled upon the rotting corpse of the goddess of liberty. Relentlessly, he has advocated a fanatical racial theory which has driven Germany back to what Professor Toynbee has called "the pagan worship of a parochial community." Assuming for 24 hours in the summer of 1934, the self-appointed role of Supreme Court of the German people, he shot down, on vague charges of treason, former comrades like Röhm and Strasser, ex-Chancellor Von Schleicher, prominent Catholic laymen, and the man who imprisoned him in 1923. Within five years Germany was re-armed, the Rhineland re-fortified, her self-confidence restored. Even the army, the stronghold of proud Junkerdom, had to bow its will to party supremacy in 1938. The Church, Roman Catholic and Protestant, has struggled to retain its spiritual freedom against the rising tide of paganism. The price has been high for men like Parson Niemöller, who has spent over two years in solitary confinement in concentration camps. "It must be Niemöller or I," says the Führer implacably. At home Hitler bestrides the German world like a Colossus, the idol of young Germany and the last hope of disillusioned middle age.

In the successive shocks to European nerves since the absorption of Austria, Hitler has demonstrated repeatedly his uncanny skill in timing a blow when his opponents are divided, and the issues have been cleverly blurred by his propaganda machine. When the conqueror entered 1938, he made an impromptu speech which in its emotional incoherence was most revealing. "Picture my feeling of emotion after such long years of faith to see it brought to fulfillment in rapid shouts of joy from this city to the leader of the Reich. Then fate must have given me a commission and it can only have been a single commission to return my beloved Fatherland to the German Reich. I believed in this divine commission. I lived and fought for it. I believe I have now fulfilled it. And you are witnesses to it."

But Austria did not exhaust the commission. Six months later Europe was brought to the verge of war over the Czech crisis. At the eleventh hour appeasement policies of British and French statesmen, pursued at the cost of Czechoslovakia seemed to have brought "peace in our time." Another six months passed and these hopes were rudely shattered by the further wanton destruction of the Czech republic, the recovery of Memel from Lithuania under duress, and the demands upon Poland for Danzig.

Then this reckless gambler with the peace of Europe encountered unexpected resistance. Poland refused to be intimidated by the drum-fire of threats from Berlin. Britain and France doggedly set to work to establish a "Peace Block" which would check further unprovoked aggression. The signs were clear that the British people would not tolerate another Munich, but Der Führer continued to proclaim that "In the last resort life belongs to those nations that are prepared to stake everything if necessary for their existence and peace." As Europe drew nearer the abyss in those anxious August days, the warning of a British Ambassador could only elicit the answer, "I am fifty years old; I prefer war now to when I am 55 or 60." And so the iron dice of war were flung upon the plains of Poland.

Another nation has been submerged under the tides of Nazism, Adolf Hitler has entered Warsaw in triumph, just as he previously rode like a conqueror through the streets of Vienna and Prague. But he has rouséd a grim determination to end the nightmare of broken pledges, ruined nations and shattered peace—in short, to destroy Hitlerism—

which no threats or promises can restrain. Before the war began Der Führer talked of returning to his true vocation as an artist "once the Polish question was settled." Twenty-five years ago another German ruler fancied himself as an artist and a conqueror—but later had to be content with chopping wood on his Dutch estate.

VI

CHANCELLOR DOLLFUSS, THE "RELUCTANT DICTATOR" OF AUSTRIA

THE great French historian Albert Sorel once wrote: "On the day when the Eastern question would seem to have been settled Europe would be confronted by the Austrian question." Of the correctness of this prophecy the events of the past twenty years have offered ample proof. The assassination of the Austrian archduke in June 1914 provoked the World War which completed the unification of the Balkan peoples. It also destroyed the Hapsburg empire and left in its stead a feeble republic. The assassination of her Chancellor on June 25, 1934, gave Europe its worst war scare since 1914, as German and Italian glared at each other across the body of Engelbert Dollfuss. Many hoped that Dollfuss by his death had created a martyr legend that would offset the ceaseless Nazi pressure from across the border. That hope has vanished and the Goliath of Germany has conquered. But history may still pay tribute to a brave though misguided man.

The empire over which the Hapsburgs ruled in 1914 included 50,000,000 people of a dozen nationalities. German and Pole, Czech and Italian, Serb and Magyar, Croat and Ukrainian jostled each other in a dual monarchy in which the Austrian-German and Hungarian-Magyar controlled the destinies of the rest. A Federal system of government, embodying a recognition of the various groups, might have saved the Hapsburgs, but that solution implied a degree of statesmanship lacking in Vienna. So the empire blundered along to its doom under the aged Francis Joseph with a policy that one wit described as "despotism tempered by slovenliness." Under it were born two men whose destinies were to clash violently. The first, Adolf Hitler, born in 1889, grew up an ardent German nationalist detesting what he called "the racial conglomeration which ruled the imperial capital." So convinced was Hitler that "this form of state can only bring disaster to the German nationality," that at twenty-three he left Vienna for Munich, and when the war came enlisted as a German volunteer rather than fight for the Hapsburgs. The second, Engelbert Dollfuss, born in 1892, the illegitimate child of a peasant girl, readily accepted his lot and without hesitation volunteered for service in 1914. His small stature of 4 ft. 11 in. (the source of future jokes about the "millimetre Metternich") caused his rejection on the first attempt, but in October he was more successful and reported for duty as a cadet.

When Dollfuss entered the barracks at twenty-two he had behind him a life of poverty and peasant simplicity. His foster-father had never taken kindly to the unwanted child and, had it not been for the intervention of the Catholic bishop of the diocese, the boy would probably never have got beyond primary school. But the Bishop, who recognized his ability, secured his admission to a secondary school at Hollabrunn, and there he spent eight years. At first young Dollfuss, whose family was devoutly Catholic, aspired to the priesthood, but later decided upon the study of law and was registered as a law student in the University of Vienna when war broke out. Among the other cadets Dollfuss showed leadership, comradeship and a real pride in the destiny of the Austrian people, for which he was later to sacrifice his life. His war service was spent entirely on the Italian front where he shared his men's hardships, gave frequent proof of his courage, and won the nickname of "Machine-Gun Dolli".

The Austria of 1919 offered a dismal prospect for any young man eager to make his way in the world. Reduced to an area no larger than Nova Scotia, stripped of all its natural resources, ringed around by tariff walls erected by its former subjects who had not forgotten their past subjection, equipped with a capital designed for a state of fifty millions and left with a republic of six, it seemed both hopeless and helpless. Many Austrians would have merged their country into Germany but the Allied governments forbade that. Hence the early post-war years were ones of starvation and desperation until the leadership of Dr. Seipel, a Catholic theologian, and the aid of the League of Nations brought a measure of stability.

In this unfavourable environment Dollfuss managed to find a place. He returned to the University to resume his law studies and supported himself by tutoring more fortunate students. Through the good offices of his own peasant people he came in touch with the organizer of a farmers' association and secured a post as secretary. This association was far-sighted enough to further his education and he spent over a year studying economics at the University of Berlin. From it he returned with a Prussian wife and a real respect for the new German republic. Until 1930 Dollfuss was concerned with agricultural problems, becoming the director of the Lower Austrian provincial chamber of Agriculture, regarded as a model by its neighbours. These years of negotiation with the government, promotion of rural co-operation, and mediation in wage disputes won for him, before he was forty, a wholesome respect as a shrewd and likeable executive that bore fruit in his appointment as President of the Federal Railways. Such a post brought him still nearer the centre of politics and he became Minister of Agriculture in a coalition government in 1931.

Had Dollfuss entered politics in calmer times his future policies might have been different. But when he joined the government the severity of the depression, which was soon to bring down the largest bank in Austria, had sharpened the already acute differences in politics. His own party, the Christian Social, was fervently Catholic, peasant, and individualist. It still believed in a parliamentary state but had to co-operate in a coalition government with a small group, the Heimatbund, led by Prince Stahremberg and backed by a private army, the Heimwehr, that was frankly anti-parliamentary, anti-Socialist and highly nationalist. Opposed to it on the right were the Austrian Nazis, allied to Hitler's party, eager for union with Germany and busy capitalizing the discontent produced by the depression. All three of these groups united in hating the Social Democratic party which had governed Vienna municipally since 1919, and had, as in Germany, been the creator of the republic. It was still the strongest single party and had a private army, the Schutzbund. All coalitions dependent upon a scanty majority, in this case of only one, lead a precarious life, and in a cabinet crisis of 1932 Dollfuss was offered and accepted the post of Chancellor. His former leader Dr. Seipel, who died shortly afterwards, said on hearing of his appointment, "Now Austria is in safe hands. I can die in peace."

When Dollfuss formed his anti-Socialist cabinet he announced "We have not taken office in order to promise mountains of gold, but to provide peace, harmony and bread for the Austrian people." He was able to secure a League loan which brought the country through the worst of its economic crisis, but peace and harmony were not in his power. It was only with the utmost difficulty that he got his legislation through a fiercely quarreling parliament and, when in a squabble over procedure its presiding officers resigned and there was no one legally capable of summoning its sessions, Dollfuss made use of the opportunity, in March 1933, to govern without it. Thus there emerged what one English writer has called the "reluctant dictator". As such the Chancellor issued the usual dictatorial decrees for licensing public meetings, censoring the press and harassing rival political parties. Such policies brought him more and more in sympathy with Prince Stahremberg's Heimwehr who were constantly urging more drastic measures to clean up "Red" Vienna. However, Dollfuss seems to have feared more the pressure from Germany, where the Nazi party had taken office in January and from which came vigorous propaganda by airplane, radio and newspaper to convert

Austria. Hitler had never concealed his belief that all Germans should be in one great German state, or his hope of uniting his "homeland" with the German "fatherland". In May Dollfuss ordered the expulsion of the German Minister of Justice who had utilized a trip to Austria for propaganda purposes, and Hitler retaliated by imposing a thousand mark visa upon the passport of any German tourist who wished to visit Austria. Fortified by three trips to Rome where Mussolini and he became close friends, and by the ovations which greeted him in London and Geneva, where audiences obviously admired the gallant struggle of this Austrian David against the German Goliath, Dollfuss(who banned the Nazi party in June) organized a Fatherland Front in the fall to create "a social Christian German state of Austria on corporative foundations with a strong authoritative leadership". The Chancellor never denied his country's German origin but insisted upon its right to a separate national existence. "Even if Austria is small and poor, it has," said he, " a right to its honour." The Socialists, now thoroughly cured of their earlier desire for union with Germany, were eager to work in a common anti-Nazi front but only upon democratic terms. These Dollfuss refused in his hatred of Socialism and of some of its leaders, and in the belief the people would rally to support his corporate state. So matters stood at the end of 1933.

Early in the New Year an Italian envoy visited Vienna and such observers as John Gunther and G. R. Gedye are convinced he came to confer on the details of the anti-Socialist coup. Italy had not forgotten the Socialist activity in exposing the illegal arms traffic from Italy through Austria to Hungary, and naturally did not object to the rise of another Fascist state. The Heimwehr were eager for such a policy and signs of pro-Nazi leanings among them may have induced Dollfuss to co-operate with them. On February 11, 1934, Major Fey, leader of the Viennese section of the Heimwehr and a member of the ministry, told his followers "I have seen Herr Dollfuss and I can tell you . . . he is now our man. Tomorrow we are going to clean up Austria." Then followed the tragic street-fighting in Vienna when the Socialists were suppressed after four days of desperate resistance. Dollfuss had triumphed but had destroyed the prospects of a return to democratic government and the most sincerely anti-Nazi group in the country. His sole reward was the Rome agreement of March which guaranteed the independence and integrity of Austria.

The assassination of Dollfuss in July 1934 may be attributed to the Nazi realization that there was no other way of getting rid of their most determined opponent. Despite an earlier attempt on his life the police had not taken adequate measures to guard the Chancellor. That the murder plot had been anticipated in Germany seems evident from the documents published by the Austrian government. Thus the official German news agency issued instructions, before the *putsch* was attempted, for the German press to use only official accounts of the news expected from Austria that day. The plot was timed for the day before Dollfuss left for another visit to Italy. News of it reached the Cabinet tardily, but in time for the members to disperse and prepare for resistance. Even then the police were inexplicably slow in appearing at the Chancellery. At one o'clock, while Dollfuss was making his way to a little-known exit, the conspirators rushed in, caught him and an attendant fumbling at a locked door, and shot him down in cold blood. No attempt was made to bind his wounds or staunch the bleeding from a hole in his throat, and even the services of a priest were denied him. By four o'clock he had bled to death muttering in his delirium "I only wanted peace, may God forgive the others." The Nazis, who had been betrayed by their leaders and did not know what to do after their preliminary success, surrendered to the government. The prompt action of Mussolini in mobilizing troops and the general horror in Europe restrained Germany and produced official regrets.

The death of Dollfuss produced a remarkable demonstration of grief and resentment in Vienna.

From all parts of the country thousands of peasants poured into the capital to do honour to their martyred leader. In an eloquent funeral address Prince Stahremberg declared "Dear true friend, comrade and leader—your death has given us life. Your death has won the victory. It has assured the independence of Austria so you will live on in the future. When happy men in a happy Austria once again sing the songs of their country your name will be mingled in those songs and the children will be taught how in Austria's hardest days and hours you won her freedom with your blood."

Under the heir to his policies, Dr. Kurt Schuschnigg, the government struggled for almost four years to maintain Austrian independence. The progressive decline of Italian support as Mussolini became embroiled elsewhere, the divisions among the democratic powers, and the destruction by Dollfuss himself of the party that had the most to gain by a free Austria, gave Hitler the opportunity in March 1938, to achieve his life-long ambition. On a Friday evening Schuschnigg said farewell to his countrymen in order to avoid the bloodshed that resistance to German invasion would have produced. His final words as chancellor were "So I take my leave of the Austrian people with the German word of farewell uttered from the depths of my heart, 'God protect Austria'." Schuschnigg refused to flee from Vienna, and is still a prisoner in close confinement, while his son is forced to join the Hitler Youth. That very day as the German troops approached Vienna, Frau Dollfuss was obliged to hurry into exile. In their hour of triumph, exultant Nazis smashed with sledge-hammers statues of the murdered Chancellor, a swastika flag was placed on the yellow sofa still stained with the blood of Dollfuss, and wreaths were placed upon the grave of his assassin with the inscription "and now you have finally won." In death as in life the little man was not to be spared the taunts of his enemies.

Wide World Photos, Inc.

BENITO MUSSOLINI

VII

BENITO MUSSOLINI, "IL DUCE" OF ITALY

AIR and light, strength and energy shine and vibrate in the infinite sky of Italy. The loftiest civic and national vision today leads this people to its goal, this people which is living in its great new spring-time. It animates my long labours. I am forty-five and feel the vigor of my work and thought. I, like the most devoted of citizens, place upon myself and on every beat of my heart service to the Italian people. I proclaim myself their servant. I feel that all Italians understand and love me; I know that only he is loved who leads without weakness, without deviation, without self-interest and with full faith."

It is almost impossible to imagine any British statesman concluding his autobiography in such a frank expression of glowing self-satisfaction and conceit. Even if he honestly felt it to be true he would not dare put it down in black and white for his fellow countrymen to read. Benito Mussolini has no such scruples and the passage just quoted appears at the end of his autobiography[1] published

[1] An American "ghost writer" was largely responsible for a work that is in places deliberately misleading. The only adequate study of Mussolini's early life is Gaudens Megaro: *Mussolini in the Making* (New York, 1938).

over a decade ago. It reflects that same supreme belief in himself as the Man of Destiny which we have previously noticed in the autobiography of Adolf Hitler. His book also parallels the latter's story of early struggles and disappointments, of war-time enthusiasm and post-war disillusion when, says Mussolini, "the leaves were falling fast on our tree of idealism." But Mussolini has completed almost twenty years of dictatorship during which his prestige has risen and waned, while Hitler's fame is increasing.

Benito Mussolini was born in 1883 in a small village of the Romagna region, noted for the turbulence and strong convictions of its inhabitants. His father was a blacksmith, an ardent and anti-clerical Socialist, who named his son after the Mexican patriot, Benito Juarez, who freed Mexico from foreign control and shot the unfortunate Emperor Maximilian. His mother was a primary school teacher with a deep love for her children. Her determination to have them get on in the world led her to send the boy to a normal school, though, as Mussolini confessed, "I had no real hunger for scholastic endeavour." The six years of study required for a teacher's diploma were not taken too seriously but they did arouse the young radical student's interests in the psychology of the mob, for which he entertained little respect. In 1902, at a salary of less than $15 a month, Mussolini began his teaching career but soon revolted against the monotony of his task. In July he set out for Switzerland, receiving, en route, news of his father's arrest as a dangerous radical in an election quarrel.

In Switzerland Mussolini had a hard struggle for existence and learned what it was to be hungry and to sleep under bridges. He worked as a casual labourer and as a mason before gaining employment on a Socialist paper. Like his father he preached Socialism and anti-clericalism, securing a following among the workers but being twice expelled from Swiss cantons. Lausanne did not lift the ban against him until his return as Prime Minister in 1922. Switzerland was then a meeting-place for Socialists of all shades of opinion, and Lenin got to know of the young radical's abilities. In post-war days he told a delegation of Italian workers, "I know Mussolini. He is a strong and hard man. It was a great pity to have let him go out of the Socialist party."

Back in Italy in 1905, Mussolini served his term of military service which he had previously evaded, surprising his officers who knew of his antecedents, by what he described as "his serenity of spirit and strength of character". His mother's death at this time still further severed home ties and, after another half-hearted attempt at teaching, Mussolini crossed the Austrian frontier to edit a

Labour paper. There he met Cesare Battisti, member of Parliament, journalist and an ardent Italian nationalist, who was to become a martyr for freedom when the Austrians hanged him as a traitor during the World War. Mussolini was expelled from Trent in September 1909, largely because of his views on religion and Socialism.

His third experience as a Socialist journalist was centred at Forli where his father kept an inn. His paper, *The Class Struggle,* took up an extreme position denouncing the government, the capitalist, and the moderate leaders of the workers, while preaching constantly the "Gordian knot of Italian politics could only be undone by an act of violence." For his opposition to the war with Turkey in 1911 when he declared "I would rather have Italy as civilized as little Denmark than as large as China," he had to serve a brief prison term. He was set free in time to attend a Socialist congress, where an eye-witness described him plunging into the arena like an enraged bull. His vehemence caught the fancy of the congress and he was elected to the party executive, soon after being appointed editor of the *Avanti* of Milan, the only Italian Socialist daily. Mussolini made a success of his post, almost trebling the circulation, and became with Malatesta, the anarchist, a hero of the radicals. His friends of Forli boasted of "our upright Duce".

The World War was the watershed of his career as it had been for Masaryk and Hitler. The Socialists fiercely opposed Italian intervention in what they regarded as an imperialist adventure. Mussolini agreed at first, though it seemed that his neutrality was at bottom anti-Austrian. In his paper he warned the government "if you make war on France you will have barricades in Italy." By October he had decided to support the Allies. Whether this change of heart was hastened by French bribes, as his enemies allege, is uncertain but it is not surprising that a friend of Battisti should clamour for war on the historic enemy. The Socialists promptly expelled him from the party and deprived him of his post as editor. Defiantly Mussolini replied: "You are going to strike at me tonight with banishment from the public squares and streets of Italy. Very well, I solemnly wager that I shall continue to speak and that in a few years the masses of Italy will follow and applaud me when you will no longer speak nor have a following." Three weeks later he started a new paper, *The People of Italy*, which still claimed to be radical but put its heart into appeals for war. At the same time Mussolini helped to organize groups, or Fasces, to agitate for intervention. Their cause he shrewdly predicted would contribute to the breakdown of Austria-Hungary, a revolution in Germany and even in

Russia. The World War would be a crucible, "in which the new revolutionary aristocracy is being prepared." Like Masaryk, he realized that the world of pre-war days had gone forever.

Mussolini was called to the colours in September 1915, and took a brief part in the arduous experiences of trench warfare in the mountains. He was promoted to the rank of corporal but his radical views prevented any recommendation for a commission. In February 1917 he was painfully wounded by the premature explosion of a trench mortar. On discharge from hospital he was allowed to return to his paper to help to revive the drooping morale of a hard-pressed people. The war had intensified his nationalism, widened his breach with Socialism, and deepened his belief in the need of discipline.

War brought victory but peace brought disappointment. Despite her sacrifice of 650,000 killed and a million wounded, Italy did not powerfully influence the decisions of the Peace Conference. Signor Orlando, the prime minister, was a member of the Big Four, but when he withdrew in a rage because President Wilson appealed over his head to the people in vain hope that Italy might be less greedy in her demands, the others placidly carried on without him. Italy secured a safe frontier at the expense of 300,000 German-Austrians, but her colonial gains were inconsiderable and she was not offered a mandate for former German or Turkish colonies as were Great Britain, Japan, France and Belgium. She experienced the mortification of seeing Greece encouraged in Asia Minor while she was ignored, and of being forced by the Albanians to evacuate their country. Along the Dalmatian coast the Croats and Slovenes, who had fought till the last for Austria, were now citizens of Yugoslavia and contesting the Italian claim to Fiume. The poet and war hero, D'Annunzio, seized the city but later had to surrender it to troops of his own country. If Italians were disappointed abroad they were embittered at home. Government was weak; five Cabinets fell in three years; the radical parties were at the peak and contemptuous of those who had been fools enough to fight; the cost of living was the highest in Western Europe and work was scarce for the hundreds of thousands of demobilized soldiers.

Barred from his old party and despising the orthodox parties, Mussolini organized, on March 23, 1919, a group of Fighting Fascists who pledged themselves "in the name of those who died for the greater glory of Italy to consecrate themselves entirely and forever to live for the good of Italy." Though Nationalist to the core the party had at first a radical platform demanding abolition of the senate, proportional representation, confiscation of war profits, and a capital levy. Their leader declared "We are positively against every form of dictatorship, from that of the sword to that of the three-cornered hat, from that of money to the masses." As it could not compete with the Communists in promises of social reform, skilfully the group turned to champion order, discipline and a greater Italy to appeal to the middle class. Their platform was less important than their purpose, to govern Italy, and they boasted of being the "gypsies of Italian politics", not being tied down to any fixed principles. Only after success came the present Fascist philosophy as expounded by Signor Rocco and others.

In 1919 the Fascists made little impression on politics, polling less than 5000 votes and not electing a single member of Parliament, while the Socialists returned 156. But the Socialists were quarrelling with the Communists, who were strong in 1919-20, and the farcical occupation by the workers of the factories discredited their cause. By 1921, as Mussolini then admitted, the "Red" menace had disappeared but its effect upon the people had been skilfully exploited by the Fascists. They then had 35 members in Parliament, their militia had been given "full liberty of action", as Signor Prezzolini says, to conduct their raids upon their opponents, and they had accepted a policy of subordination to the leader, Il Duce. After a series of party congresses, when Mussolini openly declared his loyalty to monarchy, thus removing the scruples of some ex-Generals who were in sympathy with him, plans were made for a march on Rome to compel the government to transfer power to the Fascists. The march began. The Prime Minister wished to proclaim martial law but the King declined to sign the decree and telegraphed to Mussolini in Milan to form a government. Mussolini accepted, "marched on Rome" by express train and established a coalition government on October 30, 1922. At 39 the radical of the Romagna had become Prime Minister of Italy.

At first Mussolini proceeded cautiously; not until 1924 was the electorate invited to pass upon the merits of the new regime. Not until 1925 did the Government cease to be coalition, after the murder of the Socialist deputy, Matteotti (who had made what Mussolini called "a speech of an outrageously provocative nature") had created considerable tension. Not until 1929 did Parliament become a slate of nominees approved by the Fascist Grand Council and elected en bloc by the people. Even yet there are a few senators, like Croce, who dare to speak and vote against the government in defiance of the Fascist theory "everything within the state, nothing outside the state, nothing against the state." As recently as 1932 Mussolini told the famous biographer Ludwig,

"Race, it is a feeling not a reality—no such doctrine will ever find wide acceptance here in Italy." It was possible for a Jewess to write an official biography and a Jew become Minister of Finance. Not until 1938 did the German influence further the adoption of a racial theory which persecuted the Jew and was sharply criticized by the Vatican. Like the adoption of the German goose-step, re-named the "Passi Romano", it was not a popular measure. The Fascist state has had its cudgels and castor oil, its islands as concentration camps and its Secret Police, but its ruthlessness has lacked the Teutonic thoroughness of the Nazis.

It is probable that Mussolini attained the peak of his prestige and and popularity when in 1935-36 he successfully defied the League of Nations and conquered Abyssinia. Months of preparation, a friendly accord with Pierre Laval, the French foreign Minister, and a skilful stiffening of public opinion at home by pointing to the efforts of foreigners to "strangle" Italy in applying sanctions, brought their reward. European military experts were amazed at the speed with which Emperor Haile Selassie's armies were swept aside and Addis Ababa entered in triumph. Victory was balm to the wounded pride of a nation that still remem-bered the defeat at the hands of Abyssinia forty years previously, and suspected that other nations still judged Italian military prowess in terms of

Caporetto. It was a proud and happy man who roared to the Roman crowd from a balcony of the Palazzo Venezia "The fate of Abyssinia is sealed today the 9th May, in the fourteenth year of the Fascist era. . . . Italy has her empire at last; a Fascist empire because it bears the indestructible tokens of the will and of the power of the Roman lictors, because this is the goal towards which during fourteen years were spurred on the exuberant and disciplined energies of the young and dashing generations of Italy." In the first flush of victory Italy was described as a "satisfied state," "an empire of peace," "an empire of civilization and of humanity for all the populations of Abyssinia."

These words have a wry taste today. Abyssinia has yet to prove a land of promise for hungry Italians and her people are obstinately reluctant to accept their conqueror, as the thousands of Italian troops know full well. The bills are still being presented for the cost of the campaign and occupation, which are reflected in the two special tax levies on property and share capital. Within a few weeks of victory in Africa new forces were sent to Spain to assist General Franco in "rescuing Spain from Bolshevism". But the Spanish republic fought for almost three years and Italy gained neither glory nor popularity in the bitter struggle. When the war in Spain was almost over Italian deputies shouted, in the presence of Mussolini, for Tunisia, Corsica and Nice, a demand which France quickly answered by strengthening her defences and which reacted unfavourably upon a Britain that had just accepted a treaty of friendship. Good Friday, 1939, was celebrated in Italy by the invasion of Albania, a helpless vassal state that had to lose its identity to give Italy a "victory" comparable to the German conquest of Prague. Such a gesture virtually destroyed Anglo-Italian co-operation and drove Italy into the arms of an alliance with Germany, to replace the "Axis" agreement of 1936. In this alliance Italy would obviously be the junior partner. She has also had to accept the disappearance of Austria, which Mussolini saved from Hitler in 1934. When it disappeared Il Duce contented himself with a telegram from the German dictator, "Mussolini, I shall never forget this of you." After this annexation he has had to arrange for the forcible dispersion of the German people of South Tyrol, given Italy at the Peace Conference, to remove the dangerous attraction of Germany as their next door neighbour.

After twenty years as leader of the Fascist party, Il Duce remains at the apex of the Italian pyramid, ever dwarfing his associates. It is dangerous for any other Fascist to become too popular, as General Balbo and Count Grandi ruefully discovered. Recently a young Fascist, Count Ciano, has risen to fame as Foreign Minister. Though the Italian press has been allowed to advertise his numerous visits to European capitals, observers are sceptical of his natural ability, and inclined to stress the significance of Ciano's position as the husband of Mussolini's favourite child. Perhaps in his son-in-law the aging Il Duce (who forbids the Italian press to make any reference to his age) sees the answer to the question once posed by wise old Cardinal Gasparri: "He (Mussolini) has strong will power and considerable genius. The people obey him and believe in him. But what will happen when one day he dies? Ah, no one can answer that question."

In the opening weeks of the second World War Italy has repeated her performance of twenty-five years ago. Once again, as Germany faces Britain and France her Italian ally clings to her neutrality, pursuing a policy of watchful waiting and ready to profit at the expense of the loser. A Duce who has persistently praised war and practised it on weaker peoples, has remained cautiously silent while the guns roar elsewhere in Europe. And yet in so doing Mussolini is only too well aware that he expresses the heart-felt desire of the Italian people.

VIII

RAYMOND POINCARE AND FRENCH NATIONALISM

OUR eighth national leader was also a fervent patriot, but never a revolutionary, a statesman, but never a dictator, a world figure who inspired fear, hatred, respect and grudging admiration, but never affection—Raymond Poincaré, Prime Minister and President of France. No man worked more sincerely, more assiduously, or more short-sightedly than this bourgeois lawyer, the embodiment of the minor virtues.

The key to Poincaré's career is to be found in the time and place of his birth. The time was 1860, the place Bar-Le-Duc in the province of Lorraine. At ten the boy saw his own province and home invaded by Germany and a part of Lorraine handed over to the victors. That bitter experience burnt into his consciousness. He was to tell a student audience fifty years later: "During my school years my spirit, oppressed by the defeat, unceasingly crossed the frontier which the Treaty of Frankfort had imposed on us, and when I climbed down from my castles in the air I saw no reason for existence for my generation but the hope of recovering the lost provinces." So Poincaré remained to the end of his days a "man of the frontiers" whose opinions on the Germans, as Mr. Lloyd George has picturesquely put it, "were those of a Salvation Army captain about the devil." As he lay dying Poincaré pointed out of the window of his home in Lorraine, and murmured "Some day They will come again."

Poincaré's family were of sound middle-class stock and good intellectual calibre. His father was a civil-servant and meteorologist, his brother a first-rate physicist, and his cousin a mathematician of real distinction. He himself graduated in law from the University of Paris and impressed all who came to know him by the clarity of his intellect, the remorselessness of his logic, and the narrowness of his interests. He never possessed the genial humour, the flashes of brilliance and the Celtic fire of Briand. He lacked completely the volcanic qualities of Clemenceau, who openly despised this prodigious accumulator of information. "Briand," he said once, "knows nothing and understands everything—Poincaré knows everything and understands nothing." In short, Poincaré was one of those solid, irreproachable, hard-working lawyers who forge to the front by sheer force of determination and character, a man whom thousands of cautious *rentiers* will trust and support.

By 1887 the young lawyer had made a sufficient mark to be elected to the Chamber of Deputies from his native department. There he acquired quite a reputation as an economist, and in six years had won promotion to the Cabinet at the early age of 33. A year later he was Minister of Finance but only for a brief period because of one of those periodic crises so familiar to students of French politics. For a time he served as vice-president of the Chamber but left for the Senate in 1903 where the certainty of nine years' tenure offered some compensation for poorer prospects of Cabinet rank. For some time Poincaré seemed more interested in law than politics, and became one of the leading members of the bar, while also winning elevation to the ranks of the French Academy.

Then came a diplomatic crisis which brought him back to the fore-front of politics, the "Agadir affair" of 1911. It arose from the determination of the German foreign secretary to get compensation, "trink-geld", as he called it, from France in return for permitting her a free hand in Morocco, which she had long wished to annex. The blustering sword-rattling method adopted to force this concession caused a clash between Triple Alliance and Triple Entente, and a stern warning from Britain to Germany. In the end Germany got 100,000 square miles of the French Congo and

France got Morocco, but the air was poisoned with suspicion and distrust. In England Mr. Churchill was transferred to the Admiralty, in order to put the navy on a more efficient footing for war. In France the Prime Minister, M. Caillaux, was forced to resign from office because of the revelation that he had worked behind the back of his foreign secretary for a better understanding with Germany. Poincaré, who had served on the Commission which investigated the circumstances, was invited to form a government in January 1912. He created what was called the "great ministry" with himself as Prime Minister and Foreign Secretary, an ardent nationalist, Millerand, as Minister of War, and the part-author of the Anglo-French entente, Delcassé, as Minister of Marine. A new stiffness was apparent in Franco-German relations, upon which the German Chancellor has remarked in his memoirs. As Poincaré expressed it: "I will not tolerate a second Agadir." He immediately set to work to transform the Triple Entente of Britain, France and Russia into a solid group. This policy has been described by his harshest critics such as Professor Barnes as "The Franco-Russian plot that produced the World War"; it won for him the nick-name in radical circles of Poincaré-la-Guerre. Most historians agree that this is too harsh a verdict but accept Poincaré's speech of October 1912 as a significant description of his aim: 'We must maintain all the patience, all the energy, all the pride of a people which does not want war but which nevertheless does not fear it." The naval agreement of 1912 with Russia and Britain, the loans to Russia for military purposes, the increased willingness to give Russia more support in the Balkans, the exchange of letters with Britain to clarify the relations of the two powers, the revival of three years' military service in 1913, were manifest proofs of the vigorous leadership the Lorrainer gave his country. His elevation to the Presidency in 1913 did not appreciably affect this policy for, as he told the Austrian ambassador, "I will see that a man is put in my place who will follow my policy." Yet France still remained profoundly desirous of peace and the elections of May, 1914, gave a decisive majority to the Left parties which had opposed the rise in armaments and the longer military service.

In spite of the murder of the Austrian archduke at Sarajevo the President and his Prime Minister paid a state visit to Russia in July 1914, which had been arranged months before. The visit proved of great importance in encouraging Russia to offer a vigorous resistance to any attempt on the part of Austria to destroy Serbia. As Poincaré warned the Austrian minister in St. Petersburg: "Serbia has very warm friends among the Russian people. And Russia has an ally, France. What complications are to be feared there." To his own ambassador he said later: "Sazonov (the foreign minister) must be firm and we must support him." The impression produced there and in Britain was well expressed in the observation of Sir Eyre Crowe of the British foreign office. "It is clear that France and Russia are decided to accept the challenge thrown out to them." When Poincaré embarked for the return voyage, the Austrian government, which had carefully ascertained his timetable, issued their harsh note to Serbia, intended to cause war. He was not back in France until July 29 and by that time Austria and Serbia were at war and Austria-Russian relations were growing steadily worse. Poincaré agreed with his ministers in telling Russia the following day that "France is quite prepared to fulfill all her obligations as an ally", but advised the Russians "to do nothing which might afford a pretext to Germany for either a general or a partial mobilization of her armed forces." A stronger warning might have curbed the rash Russian decision to mobilize, an act which made war almost inevitable but Poincaré was not prepared to run the risk of losing his strongest ally. The British government had still not committed itself and the President despatched a special letter to King George arguing that the "last possibility of averting danger is the language and conduct of the British government" and pleading for a declaration of unity of action with France and Russia. On the advice of his ministers King George replied, in what he called privately his "shocking letter" that "events are happening so rapidly it is difficult to foresee future developments." This evasive answer left Poincaré and his government in "a state of very great anxiety" only relieved when the German invasion of Belgium unified British opinion. Poincaré's policy had been successful. It has been described by a leading American historian as "not so much to avoid a conflict which was bound to come some day, though it would do nothing to avoid that conflict, as to make sure that France entered the war in as favourable a position as possible."

Throughout the war Poincaré played a creditable but inconspicuous part. He was advised to leave Paris when the Germans came near the capital in August 1914, and Mr. Lloyd George declares that Poincaré never forgot the humiliation of that flight; it intensified his enmity of Germany. Poincaré's most important act was the selection of Clemenceau, whom he heartily disliked, as Prime Minister in the gloomy days of 1917. Clemenceau was equally intolerant of him and once told his secretary, "Every time I saw his neat little handwriting it threw me into a fury." The

"Tiger" dominated the scene until the war was won and the peace-treaty signed. It is he whom Mr. Keynes has attacked so fiercely for the Carthaginian peace, while Poincaré reproached Clemenceau for not having been harsh enough. In fact, Foch and Poincaré, fellow-Lorrainers, worked hard but in vain to undermine Clemenceau's control of his Cabinet.

In 1920 Poincaré's term as President expired but he did not seek a life of leisure. He began in the reviews his long series of polemics against the bad faith of the Germans. He served for a short time on the Reparations Commission, until he became convinced that Lloyd George was undermining its authority by attempting to negotiate directly with Germany. He returned to the Senate to harass the early post-war governments which were feeling their way through this strange new world. In 1922 Poincaré was back in office as Prime Minister, after his old friend Millerand, who had followed him as President, had recalled Briand from a friendly conference with Lloyd George. The new Prime Minister's policy was "to uphold firmly and vigorously the Treaty of Versailles". For over two years he dominated the scene, with results disastrous to France and Europe. Britain was estranged by his refusal to co-operate sincerely in the Genoa conference when Germany and Russia were for the first time admitted as associates on a basis of equality, and by his withdrawal of French soldiers from the Chanak line when Britain and Turkey came near to war in 1922. Lord Curzon, the British foreign secretary, could do nothing with what he called "this horrid little man". When Bonar Law became Prime Minister he discovered that Poincaré was determined to invade the Ruhr valley in order to make Germany pay reparations in full. British experts were convinced that this was impossible but their compromise plans were ignored by a French Prime Minister who said openly: "One cannot deal with Germany on terms of equality and one must not expect Germany to live up to a voluntary agreement." French bayonets expelled 147,000 Germans from the Ruhr, killed 326 and ruined Germany economically. They also gave Hitler a potent source of oratory for the future. As Professor Toynbee has observed, Poincaré failed to show the wisdom of a Bismarck who kept a defeated France in isolation but encouraged her to win colonial laurels in Africa. He chose to treat the Weimar Republic as harshly as the Germany of the Kaiser. For that reason he must take his place as an architect of Hitler's Third Reich.

In the elections of 1924 the Poincaré policy was condemned chiefly because of its financial failure. Poincaré resigned and statesmen from the Left groups took office to accept the Dawes Plan and to frame Locarno. The Briand era of "good Europeans" was inaugurated. But the Left proved poor financiers, and, when the franc had fallen to 240 to the pound as against a pre-war 25, France turned again to Poincaré-La-Ruhr. In July 1926 he formed another national government and manfully set to work to balance the budget, raise taxes and stabilize the franc. The country regained confidence and gave him hearty support in the elections of 1928. In this government Poincaré was much more cautious, kept Briand as foreign minister and abstained from dangerous lone-hand enterprises.

In July 1929, overwork at last took its toll of an iron constitution and Poincaré was compelled to retire from office after one of the longest ministries in the history of the Third republic. He lived for five years a semi-invalid, twice declining offers to form a government. When he died in October 1934, Hitler had consolidated his power in Germany, the depression was ruining French finance and the era of French hegemony was at an end. Like Metternich he had dominated Europe for a time only to see his policy bring its own nemesis.

IX

ARISTIDE BRIAND AND FRENCH SECURITY

ARISTIDE Briand died in his simple apartment in Paris in 1932. His death occured during a special assembly of the League of Nations and provoked a remarkable demonstration of grief and regret for the most popular figure in League circles to date. For seven years he had been a regular attendant at Council and Assembly meetings. This man who in repose looked like a tramp, with his shock of uneven hair, stooping shoulders, heavy moustache, slightly crooked mouth from which dangled a perpetual cigarette, had become an institution. He it was who had presided over the Council when it stopped so decisively the war between Bulgaria and Greece, who had made the famous speech welcoming Stresemann to Geneva in 1926, who had launched the project for a European Federal Union in 1929 and declared in 1930 "As long as I am responsible for affairs, France will never make war." Not all Frenchmen shared the admiration of Geneva. Clemenceau's memoirs are full of sarcastic references to Briand. A President of France once declared that he would sooner summon a street-sweeper to form a Cabinet than invite him again. The Deputies and Senators overshadowed the last year of his life by selecting a blameless but essentially second-rate man in preference to him for the Presidency. Even in death he has not been forgiven. As recently as Christmas Eve, 1935, a gang of embryo Fascists attempted to saw through the bronze feet of his statue and chalked across the pedestal "Down with the League of Nations." Foreign Secretaries as well as prophets may have no honour in their own country.

Like Abraham Lincoln, Aristide Briand might have epitomized his early life by quoting the line from Gray's *Elegy,* "The short and simple annals of the poor." He was born in 1862 in Brittany of peasant stock, with that love of the sea that has been well described by Victor Hugo and Pierre Loti. Though his father was an inn-keeper and his mother a washerwoman there was a dash of noble blood in the family from the peccadilloes of a local aristocrat; the biographer Emil Ludwig has stressed this to account for some of his characteristics. In Ludwig's words, "From his Celtic ancestry he inherited the blue eyes of a sailor, fondness for rustic life and solitude, a shrinking from society and almost anarchistic tendencies. From peasant forbears he inherited his bent figure and a certain cunning. From his bourgeois ancestors came his corpulence and laziness, and from his proletarian ancestors his desire for universal improvement and his faith in the masses. But he had the hands of a typical aristocrat and a remarkably lovely voice whose tones have been compared to the sound of a violincello. His composure and delicate instincts were those of a diplomat of the old school."

Briand had his first schooling in Saint Nazaire and showed sufficient promise for his teacher to coach him privately for a scholarship with the result that he obtained entrance to the Lycée in Nantes. Here he found a warm friend and teacher in Jules Verne, who shrewdly summed him up in a novel as "not industrious but very intelligent. He was often the last but he could make his way to the fore when he applied himself. Venturesome, enterprising, pugnacious but agreeable, good-natured and easy-going, he preached tolerance and understanding." As a boy Briand wished to be a sailor but the death at sea of a favourite uncle cured him of that desire and he began without much enthusiasm to study law. His legal studies were completed in Paris in the early eighties when Socialism was beginning to revive after its suppression following the Paris Commune. It is not surprising that the boy, poor and lacking powerful connections, was attracted by its teachings. When he returned home in 1883 he prided himself upon his advanced views and helped to found and edit a radical weekly called *The Democracy of the West.* For ten years Briand stayed in Brittany, becoming a popular figure in working class circles and absorbing the theory of the general strike from a fellow journalist. Then Paris, the magnet for every ambitious man, drew him back and he entered upon a precarious career in 1893 as a lawyer's clerk and journalist. He joined the Independent Socialist party, helped Jaurès to found the paper *Humanity,* and won fame at a trades-union congress by his fervid advocacy of the general strike as the best means of increasing the class-consciousness of the worker, and bringing on the revolution.

It was not until the age of forty that, after several attempts, Briand entered the Chamber of Deputies. This was in 1902 when party passions were high over the proposed separation of Church and State. For three years Briand kept silence, studying the tricks of debate, mingling with his colleagues in the corridors, and feeling out public opinion. He was essentially a negotiator and conciliator who believed that "when the pot boils you must either sit on it or take off the lid." He wanted the pot to boil before he committed himself. When in 1905 he did speak, his qualities of tolerance, flexibility and humour were so marked that the Chamber knew it had found the man for the occasion. A year later he entered the Cabinet as Minister of Public Instruction, thereby automatically expelling himself from the Socialist Party, which would not permit its members to hold office in any government until it was the strongest single party as in 1936. For the rest of his life Briand was, despite the absence of a strong party behind him, a key figure in all the permutations and combinations that the French political system makes necessary. Over half of his Parliamentary life was spent in public office, and he broke all records in politics, being ten times Prime Minister, thirteen Foreign Secretary, four Minister of Interior, three times Minister of Justice and twice Minister of Public Instruction. His radical friends did not easily forgive his desertion of them and they were especially indignant in 1910 when he broke a railway strike by proclaiming martial law, enrolling the strikers as soldiers and then ordering them back to work under penalty of disobeying a military command. The Chamber rang with protests but Briand replied "I have restored order. Look at my hands. You do not see one drop of blood." All his life he cared little for consistency and said in his old age, "Every government contains members whose previous speeches and articles can be quoted against them. I had my youthful dreams too but I also felt responsible for the government. I am a little like a stone that has lain a long time in running water. It has lost many roughnesses but it has kept its original form."

Unlike a fellow-Celt, Mr. Lloyd George, with whom he has much in common, Briand did not win new laurels in the World War though he was in office for over half of the time and acquired his first experience in foreign affairs. He lacked the ruthlessness and driving force that Clemenceau was to supply in 1917, and, when the latter became Prime Minister, was almost in obscurity for four years. But he saw something at first hand of the horrible carnage in the defence of Verdun, the memory of which impelled him to say ten years after: "The man who then bore the dangerous honour and responsibility had been filled with such horror by the terrible slaughter that he swore to his conscience if victory were ever won and chance ever summoned him to office again he would use all his abilities and power and his whole life to further the cause of peace and prevent the repetition of such slaughter."

It would have been well for France had a negotiator like Briand been her chief delegate at the Peace Conference. Some of the bitterness which he had later to dispel might never have been created. But France was still in too nationalist a mood for Briand to be her spokesman and when he did return to office in 1921 he showed the effect of his reading of the nationalist temper of the people. At the Washington Naval Conference Briand was stubborn in his defense of the submarine, which the British wished to abolish, and would not consider any plan for the reduction of land armaments until France had been given greater security. On reparations he was more yielding because of his conviction that, as he said, when France set out like Jason to find the golden fleece of reparations she would almost certainly find only an old sheepskin. For that reason he was more ready than his predecessors to discuss with Mr. Lloyd George plans for reductions. At one conference such plans were enlivened by a game of golf in which Briand, who had never played before in his life, made the usual beginner's exhibition of himself. This gave his enemies a chance to exploit nationalist feeling and Briand had to hurry back to Paris, only to resign before a certain adverse vote could be cast against him. For three years more he was out of office, while Poincaré and his colleagues discovered that bayonets might hold Germany down but could not dig coal in the Ruhr Valley. A more liberal government called him back as Foreign Minister in April 1925, and he arrived just in time to welcome the Stresemann offer of treaty of guarantee which his predecessor had not taken seriously. With the aid of Sir Austen Chamberlain the two foreign secretaries of these age-old opponents created the Locarno agreements. In Briand's apt words, "We have spoken European, a new language that should be learned."

For the rest of his life Briand was a symbol of peace for France and the world. He really liked and understood Stresemann, despite their differences in temperament, and there was a moment in 1926 when France and Germany seemed to be entering a new partnership. Not long after his marvellous speech welcoming Stresemann to the League, predicting, "No more wars between us, No more long veils of mourning, No more sorrowing . . . No more bloodshed to settle any differences between us . . . Down with rifles, machine guns and cannon, clear the way for conciliation, arbitration and peace, (*C'est fini, la guerre*)," the two men slipped off to a country inn to draw up plans for reconciliation which might have meant the return of the Saar Valley and the freedom of the Rhineland far ahead of treaty schedule. Stresemann went home to wait for word of a new offer. Briand returned to Paris where his old opponent Poincaré had been installed again as Prime Minister in the fight to save the franc. He found the Lorrainer coldly suspicious of his plans. In Geneva he had jested, when warned "Poincaré has his eye on you,"—"Yes, as the lion has his eye on the tamer." But in Paris he was no match for him. The result was no further gesture to Germany until Poincaré was out of office two years later and Stresemann's sad reproach, "We have lost two precious years."

These two years did produce one gesture towards peace with which Briand will always be associated. In April 1927, at the prompting of Professor Shotwell of Columbia University, he suggested to the American government that France and the United States should permanently rule out war as a means of settling national disputes so far as they were concerned. This proposal Mr. Kellogg transformed into a general treaty to renounce war as an instrument of national policy and to settle all disputes by peaceful means which we know as the Briand-Kellogg Pact or the Peace Pact of Paris. After some demur Briand co-operated in the negotiations and the Pact was signed in Paris in 1928. It is doubtful if so sceptical a statesman shared the visionary enthusiasm of American peace-lovers but he undoubtedly hoped something might be made of this moral gesture.

After Stresemann died in 1929 Briand was less happy in his relations with Germany. The rise of Nazi strength in the German Reichstag from 12 in 1928 to 107 in 1930 alarmed French opinion and gave his enemies a chance to sneer at his delusions about the "new Germany". Though Poincaré had retired from politics and he seemed a fixture in the foreign office, Laval or Tardieu, when Prime Minister, were just as watchful of the interests of nationalist conservative France and in moments of crisis rather pushed Briand to one side. Such was the case during the London Naval Conference in 1930, in the negotiations over the Hoover Moratorium in 1931, and over the proposed Austro-German customs union which Briand had rashly declared to be absurd two weeks before its commencement. More and more the veteran statesman retired into the background, the symbol of a rapidly-vanishing optimism. He died before Hitler was installed as Chancellor, before Locarno was a wistful memory, and before Geneva had come to question with marked suspicion the motives and methods of a French foreign minister.

Briand must be ranked among the leaders in the second class. He was neither a great thinker nor a man of action. By temperament he could not be a visionary idealist, by training he could not be a statesman daring enough to take such risks for peace as Stresemann did. Poincaré once described him in puzzled fashion as "a poet, perhaps a mystic but so keen that he always knows to stop in time." Perhaps in his quest for peace Briand stopped too soon.

X

THOMAS GARRIGUE MASARYK, THE GRAND OLD MAN OF CZECHOSLOVAKIA

THIRTY years ago an American student of political science published a book entitled *The Irresistible Movement Towards Democracy*. No one laughed at the title or questioned the assumption. Everywhere it was taken for granted that democratic government was the logical type which every country sooner or later would adopt. In 1917, on the entry of the United States into the World War. President Wilson made a famous speech in which he declared that the world must be made safe for democracy and his sentiments were applauded to the skies. Today it has become fashionable to sneer at the blunders of democracy and to prophesy almost gleefully its imminent collapse. Three great European nations—Russia, Germany and Italy—have renounced democracy and all its works, while of the ten small states of Central and Northern Europe that emerged from the chaos of the World War only one did not experience in its early years a real or semi-dictatorship. That country was Czechoslovakia and the triumph of the democratic ideal there was largely due to the vision and leadership of Thomas Garrigue Masaryk. At the age of 84 this Grand Old man was elected for the fourth time to the presidency of his country and retained undiminished the ideals of his youth. As he told the Czech dramatist, Karel Capek, "I may say that office confirms and completes everything that I have believed and that I have not needed to change one item of my faith in humanity and democracy in the search for truth nor in the supreme moral and religious command to love men."

The career of Thomas Masaryk is a living proof of the possibility of wise leadership emerging from the ranks of the humble and meek. He was born in 1850 on the Hapsburg estates in Slovakia. His father was a serf and a coachman whose heart was never in his work because of the bitterness of servitude. As his son said, "he doffed his hat to his masters but had no affection for them." His mother was a cook of Czech descent, so that the first President of Czechoslovakia was to be an admirable symbol of the union of two peoples derived from the same Slav stock but differing in dialect like a Lancashire mill-hand and Cockney clerk. The boy's mother was determined not to have him become a drudge like his parents and saw to it that he attended school even though it required special permission before he could go on to a secondary one. At 14, his father apprenticed him to a Viennese locksmith but after three weeks' unhappiness the boy ran home to his native village. There he was apprenticed to a neighbour blacksmith and but for the shocked distress of the schoolmaster at seeing his best pupil dropping his studies so early in life, he might have been one of those village Hampdens of whom the poet has sung. Through his efforts Masaryk was sent to a school in the neighbouring town of Bruno, where he became conscious for the first time of his Czech heritage and of the patronizing attitude of the German students. In the next 17 years he studied in Vienna and Leipzig, winning his Ph.D. by a study of Plato, and attracting considerable attention by a pioneer sociological study of suicide as a phenomenon of Western civilization. While a struggling student in Vienna supporting himself by tutoring, he met a young American girl, Alice Garrigue, whom he married in 1878 after a journey to America to gain the father's consent. She encouraged his already wide reading of English and American authors, while entering fully into his love and pity for his own people who had been for two and a half centuries under the yoke of the Hapsburgs. Before the fatal battle of White Mountain the Kingdom of Bohemia had been of considerable importance in Europe. (To this day a Prince of Wales bears on his crest the three ostrich feathers of the blind King of Bohemia who fought with the French at Crécy against the Black Prince.)

In 1882 the young scholar was called to the University of Prague as Professor of Philosophy and in the ensuing 30 years won a unique place among his countrymen. From the beginning he refused to support the ignorant and narrow nationalism based upon emotion that too often passed for Czech patriotism. "What is needed," he declared, "is an inner renovation without which there is no meaning in political liberty; what is needed is an active love for one's neighbours without which there is no true patriotism; what is needed is to establish public life upon the basis of morality and truth." True to his convictions, shortly after his appointment he enraged the nationalists by proving as forgeries some manuscripts that had been highly cherished by the Czechs as evidence of their early literary achievements. On another occasion, in 1899, he successfully defended almost single-handed a Jewish pedlar against a charge of ritual murder when racial prejudice was in flames. This chivalrous gesture the Jews did not forget and they helped to smooth his path during the World War. Ten years later he was championing the cause of a group of South Slavs who were being tried for treason by the Austrian government and did not hesitate to charge high Viennese officials with forgery of documents. The fame of the scholar began to grow and on two occasions he was invited to lecture in America colleges. Twice he visited Russia and came in touch with Tolstoy. His book, *The Spirit of Russia,* published in 1913, was a scholarly achievement which still remains a standard introduction to Russian thought in the nineteenth century. Though a member of Parliament since 1907, when he headed a small group called "Realists," Professor Masaryk successfully avoided the arts of the demagogue; a German journalist described him in 1909 as "the lonely Slovak of Prague, to some a mixture of Tolstoy and Walt Whitman, to others again a heretic, to others an ascetic, to all an enthusiast." His years of contact with Vienna had convinced Masaryk of the moral and physical degeneracy of the Hapsburg dynasty and he laboured to elevate his people's condition so that they might be worthy of self-government if ever the opportunity presented itself.

The World War presented that opportunity and in the crash of conflict Masaryk felt like his great forerunner, Commenius, "I, too, believe before God that, when the storm of wrath has passed, to thee shall return the rule over thine own things O Czech people." The sight of young Czechs being marched off to fight for a cause in which they did not believe and against a Russian people whom they regarded as brothers, both angered and saddened the scholar. Of these bewildered recruits an Austrian general said in amazement, "They join the colours like lambs, they fight like lions and when we lose they are as happy as sand-boys." This tragic dilemma made Masaryk feel, as he has told us, "Since you are a member of Parliament go and do something." So at 64 the philosopher became conspirator in a struggle which caused his own flight and sentence of death while in exile, his daughter's imprisonment and his wife's illness.

Until December 1914, he managed to stay in the country while communicating with friends like Wickham Steed of *The Times,* and arranging for the Russians to welcome deserters from Czech regiments in the trenches opposite them. Twice he visited Holland to inform English scholars like Dr. Seton-Watson of the internal condition of Austria-Hungary and to urge them not to overlook the actions of the Hapsburg state in their death grapple with the Hohenzollern Empire. The Austrian authorities became suspicious and, in the nick of time, he escaped across the frontier into Italy with his youngest daughter. Through the adroitness of a pupil and brother professor, Edward Benes, he maintained contact with Prague until the early fall of 1915 when Benes had to leave as well. But a strong secret society, the Maffia, continued the good work, providing them with valuable information for the Allies and receiving in return encouraging news of Allied policy. On the 500th anniversary of the burning of John Huss, the famous Czech forerunner of the Reformation, Masaryk proclaimed in Geneva the undying determination of the Czech people to win their independence. A Czech National Council was formed abroad and remittances came from America to finance its work. Benes in Paris, Masaryk in London, and Stefanik, a young astronomer and aviator in Rome and Russia, set to work to convert the Allies to the justice of the cause. It seemed a hopeless struggle for a philosopher, a sociologist and an astronomer to pit their puny resources against an empire of 50,000,000, but they never faltered in their efforts.

The first great success was the invitation to Professor Masaryk to join the staff of the University of London and there he delivered in October 1915, his inaugural lecture, which was entitled, "The Problem of Small States in the European Crisis". The fact that Mr. Asquith, the Prime Minister, agreed to act as chairman and, when illness prevented, sent Lord Robert Cecil, gave him an entrée to important circles and checked the tendency of the London police to regard every Austrian subject as an alien enemy. In February 1916, Briand received Masaryk and was so impressed by his arguments that the Czechs were able to organize as one legion for service in the French army. Briand, again under the prodding of Benes, included in the statement of Allied war aims issued in January 1917, a clause for "the liberation of the Italians as also of the Slavs, Rumanians and Czechoslovaks from foreign domination". It embarrassed Masaryk that a committee of Czech parliamentarians in Prague, facing imprisonment and death, disavowed any desire for independence but he was able to convince the Allies of their difficult situation. In May 1917 Professor Masaryk decided to go to Russia to reorganize the thousands of Czechs there into a separate army which should be transported to the French front. His efforts brought him into the thick of the Bolshevist revolutions in Moscow and Kiev and it was not until March 1918, that he departed by way of the Trans-Siberian Railway, leaving behind him an army of 50,000 which finally won their way through to Vladivostok, in what Lloyd George described as one of the greatest epics in history. Washington was the next centre of interest for the tireless conspirator, and en route Masaryk stopped in Chicago, the second largest Czech city in the world. There he was given a great reception by his countrymen. Powerful friends made easier his access to President Wilson. Until that time the latter had not explicitly advocated Czech independence; his famous Fourteen Points only contained a reference to offering the subject peoples of Austria-Hungary "the freest opportunity for autonomous development". The philosopher's breadth of vision and grasp of principle appealed to the other ex-college professor and in September Wilson formally recognized the Czech National Council as the provisional government of Czechoslovakia, thus falling in line with the French and English, who had moved a little more quickly. On October 14th the Council organized as a Government with Masaryk as President and Prime Minister, Benes as Foreign Secretary, and Stefanik as Minister of War. Two weeks later, as the Hapsburg Monarchy was collapsing in ruins, the Czechs in Prague proclaimed their independence in a bloodless revolution. On December 21st the exile returned in triumph as first President of the Republic of Czechoslovakia.

It was a ruined country that greeted him—no bread, no railroad service, not even a regular postal system. But the Czechs have been well called the "Yorkshiremen" of Europe and grimly and doggedly this nation of 14,000,000 set to work. Of this population, over 3,750,000 were Germans and Magyars who resented the rule of their former subjects and were hopeful of failure. By degrees the majority of the Germans were reconciled to their position and in 1926 German deputies entered the Coalition Cabinet, where they remained until 1938. The triumph of Hitler and the persistent rumours of the return of the Hapsburgs caused new anxieties at the close of President Masaryk's life, but the old man remained calm and untroubled, urging his countrymen to remember that "in the development of the school lies the development of democracy, that democracy is not alone a form of state but a philosophy of life and an outlook upon the world" and advising them, "if you love your country don't talk about it but do something worth while. That is all that matters."

President Masaryk's eighty-fifth birthday was the occasion of nation-wide rejoicing. He began, however, to feel his failing strength unequal to the tasks of office, and resigned in December, 1935, to be succeeded by Benes. He continued his literary work and to receive and counsel his friends in office. He died quietly on September 14, 1937, and a week later over two million people crowded the funeral route in Prague, while the leading statesmen of Europe united in paying him honour.

So long as the Czechs can produce leaders like Thomas Masaryk no tyrant can keep them permanently in bondage. The historian of tomorrow may well hail him as one of the most far-seeing statesmen of our time and apply to him the noble words of Motley regarding William of Orange: "As long as he lived he was the guiding star of a brave nation, and when he died the little children cried in the streets." As the Czechs from the depths of defeat look back on the days of freedom they still find inspiration in Masaryk. As Senator Votja Benes wrote after his escape from Prague, "The Czechoslovakian people believe with Masaryk, the dead and eternally living leader of his country, that not Caesar but Christ will in the end be victorious."

XI

EDWARD BENES, AND THE FIGHT FOR CZECH FREEDOM

EARLY in 1917 Mr. Wickham Steed, the Foreign Editor of *The Times*, was crossing the English Channel. At Havre a Scotland Yard Inspector took him aside and whispered: "Do you know anything about a fellow who calls himself 'Beenees' sir? We don't like him here. We know he is an Austrian, yet he comes through from time to time with a Serbian passport. How can an Austrian be a Serbian? He is very mysterious and we have put a black mark against him. Whenever he turns up, though his papers seem to be in order, we run him in for a little so as to make him miss the boat. But we have never yet been able to catch him out."

Mr. Steed, who had good reason to know the suspect, replied: "My dear Inspector, 'Beenees' is a very important man. He is a friend of mine and straight as a die. You had better not run him in any more. Before very long that fellow may be signing passports which you will have to respect; and then he may tell our government that a certain Scotland Yard Inspector at Havre is a nuisance and ought to be removed. So treat him kindly."

The puzzled Inspector took the journalist's advice and one hopes that he was properly impressed by the shrewd prediction about the future of his suspect. In October 1918, "this fellow who calls himself Beenees" became Foreign Secretary of Czechoslovakia, and held that post until December 1935, when he retired to become President of his country in succession to his friend and teacher, Dr. Thomas Masaryk. Despite his new office, Dr. Benes deserved to be called the "perpetual Foreign Secretary of Central Europe" because of his unparalleled length of tenure of office and because the direction of foreign policy still remained mainly under his supervision until he resigned as President in October 1938.

Dr. Edward Benes is one of the youngest of the European leaders, and the only one whom the wheel of fortune has spun full circle back to the heavy task of re-winning freedom. He was born in a little village in Western Bohemia in 1884, the youngest in a family of ten. The family were humble, hard-working peasants who had tilled the soil for centuries but had adapted themselves to the changing conditions of agriculture. At the age of twelve young Benes went to Prague to live with a brother who was a school-teacher, and to continue his studies. Athletics appealed to him as well as books and, though he broke his leg while playing foot-ball in High School, the boy did not abandon the sport and played fullback on the Czech team in 1903. To this day the President is a keen tennis player, showing in his playing the same doggedness, resourcefulness and energy that may be said to characterize his whole career. As a college student in 1904, Dr. Benes had lectures from Masaryk, then Professor of Philosophy in the University of Prague, and the two men established a friendship that remained unbroken and created one of the most adventurous and unusual partnerships in revolution in history. The young scholar was not content to end his studies in a Central European University and with a scanty income assured him by writing for Prague newspapers, set out for Paris in 1905. For almost four years he continued his graduate studies in Paris, London, Berlin and Dijon, where he took his degree as Doctor of Laws, with a thesis bearing the significant title, "The Austrian Problem and the Czech Question." These years of travel, journalism and study proved to be invaluable in his later work as a propagandist, deepened his interest in the radical and non-doctrinaire Socialist thought which flourished in France, and created an admiration for the harmony of liberty, order and economic progress that he saw in England. Germany impressed him by its might and efficiency but the Czech was painfully affected by "the atmosphere of constraint and the prevailing influence and authority of the military, aristocratic and bureaucratic castes". Yet even it stood in favourable contrast to Austria-

Hungary, as the attempt of the Austrian autocracy to govern a multi-national state was neither efficient nor popular. Travel and study had only deepened the scholar's early sentiments as a young Czech patriot and made him in his own words "a convinced radical and revolutionary".

In spite of his dissatisfaction with the existing order, Dr. Benes did not embark on the career of an agitator. He declined the offer of a journalistic post and plunged into further study preparatory to his career as a University lecturer. Though he never abandoned the hope of a political career he took no active part in politics in pre-war days, contenting himself with supporting the Progressive or Realist party which Masaryk had founded, and which avoided the extravagances of other Czech national movements. The World War ended the career of a promising sociologist and political scientist who had believed for some time that Britain and Germany would have to fight, but thought that Austria-Hungary, because of her internal weakness, would avoid a conflict. When her leaders blundered into war Benes thought from the outset that it meant the doom of the Hapsburg empire. "Now that the fateful moment had arrived I began with a calm mind, determined to go to any length and to sacrifice everything to carry out a revolution."

It was an immense relief to him when early in September 1914, he discovered that Masaryk shared his sentiments. The two men met on the street and the young lecturer could not help pouring out to his colleague his hopes and aspirations. He ended by saying "Something must be done." To his joy the veteran scholar, then 64, replied, "I am already doing something." The younger man promptly offered his services and showed his sincerity by making a contribution from his small income to finance the underground work of conspiracy. The following month Dr. Masaryk journeyed to Holland where he established contact with English and French friends like Mr. Steed, Dr. Seton-Watson and Professor Denis. On his return a small group of the Realist party met to hear his report on the situation as viewed in Western Europe and formed a revolutionary association called the Maffia. Masaryk had already secured help from an agent who copied documents in the Ministry of the Interior's office in Vienna and one of Benes's first tasks was to travel back and forth from Vienna with information secured from this spy and to smuggle foreign papers across the border from Dresden. Dr. Masaryk went abroad again in December and during his absence the Vienna agent warned the Maffia that the police were waiting to arrest him when he returned. Benes, who had been placed in temporary charge of the group, managed to get to Switzerland in time to head off Masaryk and it was agreed that he should establish a messenger system with the exile, who would keep them informed of developments elsewhere. Benes was asked to send his brother to the United States to raise funds among the million or more Czechs there. The arrest of three of the leading members of the Maffia in the summer of 1915, and the warning from spies among the police that his turn was coming, put an end to Benes's perilous work in Prague and drove him hurriedly across the border in September 1915.

For three years Dr. Benes made his headquarters in Paris, where he was secretary of the Czechoslovak National Council which had branches in England, Italy, the United States, and Russia. His pre-war connections with French journalists and scholars and his experience as a journalist were useful in his patient campaign to persuade the French government that this revolutionary movement should be encouraged in its fight against the Hapsburg empire, and that it might even be valuable in recruiting soldiers to fight with the Allies. The first diplomatic success came in January 1917, when, after Benes had had an interview with Briand, the Allied Governments consented to include among their war aims, as outlined in a note to President Wilson, the freedom of the Czechoslovaks from foreign domination. This concession was in danger of becoming valueless later in 1917 when the Austrian government attempted secret negotiations for a separate peace and found sympathy in high quarters, but the accession of Clemenceau to office in November ended the possibility of what Benes calls in his memoirs "an unmitigated disaster". The next month Clemenceau approved the existence of a separate Czech army, flying its own flag but recognizing the authority of the French supreme command, and Benes began to fill its ranks from the prisoners of war on the various fronts, the Foreign Legion and the volunteers who came from the United States. With obvious feeling he writes in his memoirs "I still recall with emotion that memorable ceremony at Darney on June 30 (1918), the spectacle of our troops marching past the President, the Ministers and the Generals, and proclaiming their vow, the officers with drawn swords and the rank and file by raising the fingers of their right hand, that they would return home as freemen or die on the French battlefield. . . . It was at Darney that for the first time I felt confident of victory." This event took place while Masaryk was in Russia and the United States, organizing the movement there, and was followed in August by a letter from the British Foreign Office recognizing the National Council as the present trustee for the future Czechoslovak government. Such recognition, which was paralleled by similar action from the other Allied Powers, was of the first importance as it gave the Czech leaders official status as belligerents before Austria-Hungary could follow the German example of negotiating with President Wilson on the basis of the Fourteen Points. When it did commence discussions Benes had still further secured his country's position by having France recognize on October 14 a Czech National Government with Masaryk as President and himself as Foreign Minister. President Wilson, who had been greatly impressed with Masaryk, warmly approved of this step, and in despair the Austrian government allowed some Czech leaders in Prague to visit Geneva to meet Benes and some of his colleagues. This meeting on October 26 unified national action and two days later the people of Prague celebrated their independence with complete impunity. The Hapsburg empire had passed into history.

Dr. Benes must have been sorely tempted to return home but he knew it was essential to defend the diplomatic front in Paris and hurried back to secure admittance on November 4 to the Supreme Military Council. It was a proud moment. "Three years previously I had escaped across the frontier of Bohemia, crawling through the thickets to avoid being seen by the Austrian and German gendarmes and staking the whole future on what destiny might bring. Now I was sitting in conference with the representatives of France, Great Britain, the United States, Italy, Japan, Serbia, Greece,

Belgium and Portugal to decide with them as to the fate of the empires of Wilhelm and Karl." It was not until September 1919, that his work at the Peace Conference was over and he could re-enter Prague, welcomed by half a million of his countrymen and greeted almost as a son by the President. "Four years of toil and struggle abroad, in which there had been no respite and no moment without anxiety, were ended."

Peace though signed was not assured. There were boundary troubles with Poland and Hungary. Revolution and reaction which threatened the new governments in Austria, Hungary and Germany might well menace the safety of the new state with its large German and Hungarian minorities. Dr. Benes hastened to conclude a treaty of alliance with Yugoslavia in 1920 to safeguard their mutual interests from any Hapsburg *putsch*. The wisdom of this course of action was demonstrated the following year when the Emperor Karl made two attempts to return to the head of the Hungarian government. Had it not been for the vigorous action of Czechoslovakia, and the adherence of Rumania to the policy of the other "succession states", which resulted in the appearance of the Little Entente, the Archduke Otto would not have been obliged to live in exile. As he well knows, the slight form of Dr. Benes was before Hitler the greatest obstacle to his return—"our best army", as an American observer reported that people in Prague declared with pride.

For 15 years President Benes had an unequalled experience in attending every major international conference whether in Geneva, London or Locarno. His skill as a negotiator and master of international procedure was repeatedly recognized. He took a leading part in 1924 in drafting the Protocol of Geneva which, though still-born, is a landmark in the organization of peace. The British and Persian governments were able in 1933 to compose quietly their differences in the dispute over the Anglo-Persian oil company through his tactful efforts as mediator. When the League Assembly in 1935 needed a veteran chairman in the crisis created by Italy's policy it was Dr. Benes whom they elected and who had later to summon the historic session when Italy was declared the aggressor.

When President Benes succeeded his revered master and teacher Czechoslovakia was still a fortress of freedom in Central Europe, a living proof that Democracy could govern as efficiently and more fairly than any dictatorship. But three million Germans, who had lived in Bohemia for centuries, were stirring restlessly under the influence of the heady doctrines of racial unity preached by Konrad Henlein, who was to show later how faithfully he had obeyed "his Master's voice". Perhaps it might have been possible to come to terms with Germany in 1936 when various hints came from Berlin. The President, who had as Foreign Minister negotiated an alliance with Soviet Russia, subsidiary to the Franco-Soviet one, decided to remain loyal to his friends, while declaring that his government "always aimed at keeping a good entente with all States without discriminating between their régimes, or their internal policies, or the parties in power." As the clouds grew darker Benes told an interviewer "Czechoslovakia will rely upon the loyalty of her allies, while making every reasonable effort to satisfy the wishes of her German minority, and to placate Germany." His government laboured steadily, if slowly, to redress the grievances of the Sudeten Germans of whom Anthony Eden was to say in October 1938: "there is no German minority in Central or Eastern Europe that is enjoying today privileges equal to those the Sudeten Germans always had."

When Hitler annexed Austria on March 13, 1938, the red light of danger flashed in Prague. Although General Göring promptly told the Czech ambassador in Berlin that "it would be the earnest endeavour of the German government to improve German-Czech relations," the Czechs were not deceived. Their partial mobilization two months later slowed down the German drive and drove

Hitler into one of those fits of vindictive rage that have so often spelt ruin to his opponents. As he shouted to his followers at Nüremberg, "the problem is not that of Czechoslovakia but of Doctor Benes."

All through the anxious summer of 1938 the Czechs remained quiet and collected, with their President urging them as he did in a broadcast in early September, "to preserve our calm and our belief in ourselves, our state and its happy progress," while "ready for all sacrifices". Then came the dramatic surprise of Prime Minister Chamberlain's flight to Berchtesgaden and the subsequent Anglo-French decision to avert a possible European war by a "rectification" of the Czech-German frontiers. Even then by the increasing harshness of his demands Hitler almost gave the Czechs a chance to fight for their freedom. The Munich conference destroyed this prospect. With Poland and Hungary joining in the scramble for territory, Britain and France proclaiming "peace in our time", and any chance of Russian aid being ruled out by the dislike of the Czech Agrarian party of such support, resistance was hopeless. The break-up of Czechoslovakia commenced, and prodded by German bayonets, the unhappy country entered the path that led to its ruin in March 1939.

In the hour of defeat Edward Benes displayed no bitterness or rancour. He resigned as President to make it easier for his people to adapt themselves to new conditions. As he told them in a farewell message: "Do not expect a single word of recrimination in any direction. History will one day pass its verdict and decide justly." Then he retired into exile without complaint, to re-enter after an absence of almost twenty-five years the lecture-halls of a university—but this time in the New World.

The destruction of Czechoslovakia drew from the exile in Chicago a flaming message. "Before the conscience of the world and before history I am obliged to proclaim that the Czechs and Slovaks will never accept this unbearable imposition on their sacred rights, and that they will never cease their struggle until these rights are reinstated for their beloved country." At 55 as at 30 this patriot is rallying his countrymen abroad to prepare for the day when the Czechs and Slovaks will be free again.

When Britain entered the second World War Dr. Benes pledged his people to march with Britons in the struggle for a free Europe and the liberation of their Fatherland. His offer was welcomed by the British government and Czech legions are once again rallying for freedom.

XII

KING ALEXANDER AND THE UNIFICATION OF YUGOSLAVIA

THE old adage, "Uneasy lies the head that wears a crown," especially applies to the rulers of Serbia, and its successor, Yugoslavia. Since the struggles in the early nineteenth century for Serbian independence, of its dozen rulers, four have been murdered, four were forced to abdicate and one through failing health was compelled to transfer the real power to his son for the last seven years of his reign. The latest, and let us hope the last, of these royal crises took place in October 1934, when King Alexander was murdered at Marseilles just as he had set foot on French soil. If he had lived this visit might have seen his greatest achievement.

The death of "the knightly King Alexander, the Unifier", as he was termed in a League of Nations resolution, ended abruptly the career of the only king-dictator in Europe. Like Albert of Belgium he shared the sorrows and triumphs of his people from the bitterness of defeat and occupation by the enemy to the joys of unification and victory. Yet, like Dollfuss of Austria, he became the victim of an explosion of frenzied fanaticism which found its victim though it failed in its purpose.

King Alexander was born in Montenegro in 1888 where his father, the future King Peter of Serbia, had taken refuge. He belonged to the Karageorgevitch family and was a great-grandson of the famous Black George, who led the fight for freedom in 1803, and was murdered by the head of the rival noble family, Obrenovitch. This murder created a blood feud between the two families which helps to explain the turbulence of Serbian history. The murder of the ablest of the Obrenovitch rulers in 1868 was the reason for the birth of Alexander in exile. His mother was a Montenegrin princess, daughter of the crafty Prince Nicholas, from whom Alexander is said to have inherited some of his fondness for personal rule and gift for intrigue. Despite the pettiness of the Montenegrin state Prince Nicholas had succeeded in marrying three of his daughters into the Russian and Italian royal families, one of them being the present Queen of Italy. Alexander's mother died when he was only two and his father left Montenegro to take up life as an obscure political exile in Geneva. There he found employment as a translator and teacher of languages, revealing his personal views by translating into Serbian John Stuart Mill's famous essay on "Liberty". In a preface to his translation the future king declared "The nation which is incapable of winning its parliamentary freedom is unworthy to live."

The shabby life of a refugee rather shocked Alexander's other relatives and they induced the father to have the boy sent to St. Petersburg where his aunts could supervise his education in a more noble fashion. They secured his admission to the select list of pages to the Tsar, and the boy spent ten of the most impressionable years of his life in the most autocratic court in Europe. That experience undoubtedly left its impress and also accounts for Alexander's warm reception of Russian exiles after the revolution, and his refusal during his lifetime to recognize the Soviet government. He was still at the Tsar's court when his father was recalled in 1903 to become ruler of Serbia after the assassination of the reigning king and queen, the last of the Obrenovitch line. In this murder King Peter had no part. It was the work of a clique of army officers disgusted with the private life and political policies of the rulers. One of them, a young lieutenant nicknamed "Peter the Door" for his part in the conspiracy, was to be Alexander's right hand man in the crisis of 1929. In 1909, shortly after Prince Alexander returned to Belgrade, he was made the heir to the throne, his elder brother having been found unsuitable for the post. Three years later he had his first taste of battle when Serbia, Montenegro, Greece and Bulgaria declared war on Turkey in order to free those of their countrymen still under the rule of the "terrible Turk". The war ended victoriously but was embittered by the interference of the Great Powers who claimed the right to allocate the spoils of victory in order to safeguard their own interests, and by the action of Bulgaria in making war with her allies when disappointed in the territory ultimately assigned to her. Serbia had doubled her size in 1913 but the more feverish of her nationalists now dreamed of a day when their kinsmen under Austrian sovereignty might join in a greater south Slav kingdom. Such a policy could be achieved only through the collapse of Austria-Hungary and that state, aware of the danger, would have attempted a preventive war in 1913 if it had not been for the vigorous opposition of her allies, Germany and Italy.

On June 28, 1914, the 525th anniversary of the fatal Battle of the Field of the Blackbirds, when Serbia went down to defeat before Turkey, a day observed as one of national mourning, the heir to the Austrian throne visited the town of Serajevo, capital of the Austrian province of Bosnia which was peopled by Serbs. There he was murdered by a young student, one of a group of conspirators who had been aided and abetted by the Black Hand Society of Serbia, founded by those who planned the murders of 1903; its chief was a staff colonel. This society was at odds with the Government and was later suppressed and its leader shot in 1917. But its agents were everywhere in the administration and, despite government suspicions of the plot, managed to smuggle the conspirators, whom they had trained in Belgrade, across the frontier. The crime could scarcely have come at a worse time for the administration. King Peter had just retired from ill health and Alexander, only twenty-six, was regent, while the country was still recovering from the strain of the Balkan wars. Austria, though unaware of the full details of the plot, was determined to seize the opportunity to weaken her enemy, feeling as one diplomat said, that "Better a fearful end than endless fears." And so the Great War began.

Prince Alexander lived with his army throughout the entire war except for brief state visits to Paris and Rome in 1916. He shared with them the terrible winter retreat of 1915 across the Albanian mountains into exile, when German, Austrian and Bulgarian troops over-ran the country. The ragged, hard-bitten survivors were reorganized on the island of Corfu and played their part in the breakthrough on the Macedonian front in 1918. With them marched the Prince Regent who was, in the hour of victory, as one of his harshest critics, Louis Adamic, has admitted, "the most popular figure who had ever held power in that part of the Balkans". Serbia rejoiced, not only at deliverance, but at the collapse of her enemies, Austria, Bulgaria and Turkey, and the eagerness of the Serbs, Croats and Slovenes, who had been under Austria-Hungary, to become part of a new state. Amid great enthusiasm Alexander accepted the leadership of the new kingdom of the Serbs, Croats and Slovenes in December 1918.

Unfortunately, the new nation did not dwell long in harmony. The Serbs, a peasant people of Greek Orthodox faith and Eastern culture, who had known 350 years of subordination to Turkish despotism, lacked the statesmen to rule a nation treble the size of pre-war days. They saw themselves as the lawful masters of a country purchased by their blood. The Croats and Slovenes, more urban, better educated, brought up as Roman Catholics with Rome, Vienna and Budapest as their cultural capitals, and used in Croatia at least to a measure of autonomy, expected partnership in a free union. To their dismay the old time Serb politicians presented them with an exaggerated centralization which was not even efficient. The great champion of Croat autonomy was Stephen Raditch, a man idolized by thousands but described by an American critic as "a wrongly bound book composed of pages individually reasonable but inconsecutive". The tide of party passion led to the tragedy of June 1928, when a government deputy, exasperated by a bitter oration from Raditch, emptied his revolver into the crowd of Croat deputies. Two died instantly while Raditch was mortally wounded. The action of King Alexander in visiting his death-bed possibly averted civil war, but the Croat deputies left Parliament vowing never to return until the government was reformed, and declaring "This state is no longer a state but two states; the only button between them is the king." After six months of confused government and a series of interviews with the various political leaders, which convinced him of the gravity of the crisis, the king decided to cut the Gordian knot by assuming power himself. He did so, well aware of the risk, telling a French journalist later, "Whether I succeed or not in my task it is my own person which is at stake." On January 6, 1929, he issued a proclamation dissolving parliament and annulling the constitution of 1921. His people were told "the hour has come when there must no longer be any intermediary between the people and the king." He censured "blind political passions" for hindering the progress of national unity and urged the necessity of exploring new trails. Later he promised the country would be given "a real parliament and a real democracy by means of a real franchise". As his chief adviser the king chose the commander of his royal guard,

General Zivkovitch, "Peter the Door", and he formed a non-party cabinet.

There can be no question of the earnestness and industry with which Alexander took over the task of administration. No sovereign could have worked harder or more sincerely for the welfare of his country. At first many western friends of Yugoslavia (South-Slavia), as the country was officially renamed to avoid any invidious arrangement in order of precedence among the peoples, were ready to suspend judgment upon this experiment in dictatorship. But as time went by, the familiar features of dictatorship became more and more visible with discussion curbed, the press censored, political opponents imprisoned and arbitrary decrees issued wholesale. One of Yugoslavia's greatest champions, Dr. R. W. Seton-Watson, declared in December 1931: "In a word this régime has instituted a system of political terrorism and repression which throws utterly into the shade the worst methods ever employed by Austria-Hungary towards Croatia and the Southern Slavs in the pre-war period; and I say this quite deliberately as one who was specially active in criticizing that vanished régime, and who has remained all too long silent under the dictatorship hoping against hope that it would abandon these methods and keep its original promise." Though the kingdom received a new constitution and parliament, the dice were obviously loaded against the opposition and the elections of 1931 were boycotted by a considerable section of the population.

Force in government begets violence in opposition. Among the Croats one small group decided to use terroristic methods, and from abroad planned a series of attacks upon the government. They got in touch with Imro, the Macedonian revolutionary association, which operated from Bulgarian soil in its struggle for a unified Macedonia and had long opposed Belgrade. When King Alexander and King Boris of Bulgaria exchanged friendly visits in 1933 and the difficulty of retaining a terrorist organization on Bulgarian soil was much increased, the Macedonian revolutionists were all the more eager to aid the Croat terrorists. One of their number, Vladimir Georgieff, was told by his leader "Now you go with your brothers the Croats. It is the same battle only a different front. The enemy is the same." Alexander was well aware of the danger but had become a fatalist. As he told a famous Croat sculptor who urged greater precautions: "I know it may happen at any moment. We must be ready for it. They are wrong if they think that by killing me they can kill Yugoslavia. I am only a man and many have built before me. It will only be the stronger if I fall for it."

This tragic prophecy was justified by events. In October 1934 Alexander sailed for France to discuss with its foreign minister plans for peace in the Balkans, with France and Italy reconciled and the rights of Yugoslavia respected. He had already played an active part in creating the Balkan entente and in winning Bulgarian friendship, so much so that *The Times* declared after his death "it is to his credit that the Balkans have become more peaceful than at any time during the last sixty years." His assassins were waiting for him, in Marseilles, Paris and London. Through the laxity of the French police they got their chance at Marseilles. No one who saw the famous newsreel can forget the strained look on Alexander's face as he entered the fatal automobile, the audible sigh as he settled in his seat, and the sudden slump of the lifeless body after his murder. As he died his last words were said to have been "Protect for me Yugoslavia." That dying request has been fulfilled as the nation stands solidly against any attempt at disintegration of the state. Perhaps as much by his death as his life King Alexander earned the title of "Unifier".

XIII

NIKOLAI LENIN AND A COMMUNIST WORLD STATE

IN 1909 a Danish business man met at a tea in Switzerland a number of Russian exiles. He noticed among them a short thickset man with a dome-like forehead, deep set slanting grey eyes and a short reddish beard, to whom the others listened with the greatest deference. He spoke so calmly of his program when he returned to rule Russia that the Dane commented "I notice that you make no mention of the Tsar." "Oh," was the reply, "if the Tsar does not accommodate himself to my system he must find some nail from which to hang himself." That night the Dane noted in his diary, "I met a Mr. Ulyanov, a terrible man who intends to be master of Russia."

The terrible man is better known to us as Nikolai Lenin, a pseudonym first used by his elder brother during exile.

Vladimir Ilyitch Ulyanov was born in 1870 in the town of Simbirsk. He came of middle-class family, his father being a school inspector who rose to the lower grade of nobility for his services, and his mother a doctor's daughter who owned a small country estate. As a schoolboy Lenin won warm praise and on graduation from high school his headmaster, who, by a strange chance, was the father of the Kerensky whom he drove out of power thirty years later, made the following notation on his report. "Extremely talented, always industrious and accurate, Ulyanov has been awarded a gold medal as the most distinguished scholar in achievement, development and conduct." But the prospect of a brilliant career was blighted this same year, 1887, by the hanging of his elder brother Alexander, then a student in St. Petersburg, who was involved in a plot, which miscarried, to murder the Tsar. He belonged to a small group of revolutionary idealists who believed that "Terror is the sole form of defense that is left to a minority." Lenin had already been interested by his brother in revolutionary ideas but this event hardened his attitude though he felt that terrorism was not the right weapon in their cause. His wife tells us that he also never forgot how the supposed liberals in Simbirsk drew away from the stricken family and how none of them would accompany his mother, just recently a widow, to see her son before his death. It is therefore not surprising that as the members of the family became old enough they took their places automatically in the ranks of the underground opposition.

When Lenin entered the University of Kazan the police were on the alert and secured his expulsion before the first term ended because he took part in a student political demonstration. They also barred his entrance to any other university and it was not until 1891 that he was permitted to study law as an external student at the University of St. Petersburg. The enforced absence from college gave him an excellent opportunity for the study of the Marxian theory and when he arrived in St. Petersburg, ostensibly as a budding lawyer, he was already known to radicals as one of the ablest Russian students of Marx. In the capital he soon linked himself with the left wing Marxians among whom was his future wife and devoted comrade, Nadezhda Krupskaya. They established the Union for the Struggle for the Emancipation of Labour and began to agitate among the workers. Characteristically, Lenin, who never divorced theory from practice, published as his first pamphlet a study of the system of fines in the factories (to arouse the workers against their exploitation). This again brought the police down on him and he had to go into hiding. Because of ill health he was allowed to go to Switzerland in 1895 and there he met Plekhanov and Axelrod, who were the leaders of the revolutionary movement. The young man impressed them as one who "knows what he wants to do and how it is necessary to do it" and they sent him back to edit a worker's paper. This the police promptly seized and kept Lenin in close confinement for a year before his trial. The enforced leisure was utilized to begin his most scholarly work, *The Development of Capitalism in Russia,* which caused the greatest Russian economic historian to say later "What a fine professor might have been made out of Lenin."

Found guilty of conspiracy, Lenin was sentenced to three years' exile in Siberia, where he lived in a peasant's hut in a small village. The time was spent in furthur study, in translating a book of the Webbs', and in constant correspondence with his associates who founded during his absence the Social Democratic Party. When his term was up the party sent him abroad to act as one of the editors of a new paper, *The Spark.* For seventeen years with one brief interval he and his wife were to live in obscure colonies of Russian exiles in Munich, London, Paris and Geneva, plotting, scheming and wishing for the revolution. In London, Lenin spent hours of study in the British museum and in his walks and talks learned more of the seamy side of life there than many English Marxians. There Trotsky first met him and he tells us how Lenin showed him Westminster Abbey and remarked grimly "That's a fine Westminster theirs"—"theirs" meaning the possessing classes whom Lenin despised, as Zinoviev said later, with "a hatred as keen as a sharpened sword".

In exile Lenin waged a threefold war against Tsardom, against those who wished to develop the working class movement along trade-union lines, and against those who would enter in a coalition with liberals to win victory. He envisaged the party as controlled by a select group of trained revolutionists, since, as he wrote in the first issue of *The Spark,* "Never has a class attained power without political chiefs, without men capable of organizing and leading the movement. Therefore not too much democracy in the internal organization of the party, but above all leaders and better still one leader." This attitude caused the famous split in 1903 when a small majority of the Bolshevists carried a resolution on party policy in accordance with Lenin's views against the minority or Menshevists.

This split in the party weakened its effectiveness when revolution broke out in 1905 after the defeats in the Russo-Japanese war. Lenin came home in November to help his party seize power but had to remain in obscurity because of the police. When the army downed the Moscow workers he went underground again in Finland where the police were less effective. When the last revolutionary embers flickered out he returned to Geneva feeling, as he told his wife, as if "I had come here to lie down in my grave."

It took years to rebuild the party but by 1912 it had a paper in St. Petersburg, *Pravda,* six members in the Duma or Parliament (of whom one was a police spy), and a series of cells in every industrial centre. As a police report said "The most energetic and audacious element ready for tireless struggle, for resistance and continual organization is that element, that organization and those people who are concentrated around Lenin."

When war broke out the exile was living in an obscure Galician village but was promptly arrested as an enemy alien. An Austrian Socialist leader secured his freedom and he moved to Switzerland. Lenin's frequent contacts with other European Socialist leaders at meetings of the Second International had led him to hope that they would lead their parties in opposition to war in accordance with the anti-war resolutions he had helped to draft. In this he had underestimated the cohesive force of nationalism but the shock did not change his opinion. His *Theses on the War* published in November 1914 declared that "He is no Socialist who in the time of the Imperialist war does not desire to defeat his own government, does not fight with his own chauvinists, with the imperialists of his own bourgeoisie and government." Only a handful of left-wing Socialists accepted these views at conferences held in Switzerland in 1915-16. Lenin never despaired of the eventual truth of his position but did grow gloomy about the immediate present.

Early in 1917 he told a meeting in Zurich "We of the older generation may not live to see the decisive battles of this coming revolution."

Then came the astounding news of the collapse of the Tsarist régime in March 1917, and the transfer of power to a democratic government formed by a coalition of all opposition parties. Not a single prominent Bolshevist was at hand to spur on the revolution among the soviets or soldiers' and workers' councils that were appearing. Lenin was in a fever of impatience to get back to Russia. Since he could get no passport from the Allies the only route lay through Germany and Sweden. This way was at last secured. As Lenin knew, it laid him open to the charge of being a German agent but haste was essential. Meanwhile in the Russian capital Kerensky told his government colleagues "Just you wait; Lenin himself is coming. Then the real thing will begin." Though Lenin half expected arrest no one yet dared touch this almost mythical leader of the workers' party and when his train pulled into St. Petersburg on April 3 he was given a tremendous ovation. That arrival Professor Toynbee has described as one of the decisive events in the history of our Western civilization.

Lenin was first given a bouquet of expensive flowers, which embarrassed him, and then urged in a speech of welcome to join in defending the new revolutionary democracy against every kind of attack. He brusquely ignored the handclasp of the greeter, and turning to the crowd hailed them as the advance guard of the international proletarian army which was to bring about the world-wide socialist revolution.

The next day Lenin began to educate his party. It must not support the new Republican government. It must work through the Soviets to teach the people not to trust the compromisers who would continue to support an imperialist war and a capitalist system. His followers were amazed and almost hostile. It took six months to convince the party and the people and then only after one premature rising, a hopeless offensive against the Germans, and an attempt at a military *coup d'état* from the Right. But victory came in November to the one party greedy for power led by a man with nerves of steel. Scarcely were they in office before the democratic government of their predecessors had been swept into the dust-bin of history. Lenin next shocked his party by insisting upon peace with Germany, no matter what the price might be. He was willing, as he told an enraged crowd, to make a shameful peace, to surrender St. Petersburg, Moscow or Russia west of the Volga, in order to save the Revolution and the soldiers of the Revolution, whose deaths in war would only pave the way for a restoration of the old régime. Peace was made with Germany, the Allies were estranged, but the common man, who had voted for peace by running away from the front, approved. Next came two years of brutal civil war, embittered by the attempt to murder Lenin in August 1918, which left him seriously wounded, and by the intervention of foreign powers whose support did the White armies more harm than good. By 1920 the Communists were firmly in the saddle and Lenin decided to punish the Poles for their policy by a counter-invasion which might advance Bolshevism further westward. Polish Communists warned in vain, and at what has been called the eighteenth decisive battle of the world the Red army was defeated. Peace was signed and Lenin turned to face domestic problems. For the third time he made his party bow to his judgment and abandon the War Communism which had helped to destroy the economic fabric of the country. The New Economic Policy of March 1921, or NEP, restored, as Lenin said, "a stimulus, an incentive and a push" to the small farmer by letting him sell his surplus grain on a free market after a food tax. It allowed the small shop and the small factory to reopen. But it left to the state the "commanding heights" of banking, transport, foreign trade and heavy industry. As the leader said in his last pamphlet, written May 1923, "We, of course, have not yet established a Socialist society but we have all the means required for its establishment."

NEP was Lenin's last great contribution to Communist policy. From overwork his health gave way at the end of 1921 and during the enforced convalescence the following year he suffered a paralytic stroke. From it he seemed to be recovering when a second stroke brought death in January 1924. So ended the career of the greatest conspirator in history, whose place in the ranks of the Communist party was, as Trotsky said, incomparable.

XIV

JOSEPH STALIN AND THE SOVIET DICTATORSHIP

A FEW summers ago Lady Astor, accompanied by Bernard Shaw and Lord Lothian, paid a visit to Soviet Russia. Such a distinguished group was given the rare honour of an interview with Stalin. Lady Astor began her conversation with the question: "How long will you go on killing people?" Stalin's answer was as frank as her question: "As long as it is necessary". The truth of that statement had grim confirmation between 1935 and 1938 when Russia was subjected to a blood purge, as deadly as Hitler's in 1934 but more prolonged and more widespread. As a consequence Russian prestige, which had risen rapidly, declined, the famous Red army lost eight of its most distinguished leaders, the popular belief that "Old Bolshevists" might be punished but never executed was exploded and the people experienced the greatest tension and fear since the Civil War. What has happened makes even more important an understanding of the character and personality of the party dictator, Joseph Stalin.

The word, Stalin, which means steel, was the latest of the many aliases of the present master of

Acme

JOSEPH STALIN ADDRESSING A GATHERING IN MOSCOW

the Kremlin, during his twenty years of struggle as a revolutionary conspirator. Like Lenin, Trotsky and Zinoviev, he was forced to adopt various pseudonyms while keeping under cover. Stalin's real name is Joseph Djugvashvili. He was born in December 1879, the fourth and only surviving child of a Georgian cobbler and his wife. The fact that he is not a native Russian but the son of a conquered people of Asiatic origin, one who never spoke Russian until his 'teens, has been strongly emphasized by several of his biographers. Almost certainly it helps to explain his interest in minority groups and tolerance of their language and customs so long as they accept the Soviet economic system. It may account for the crudeness and harshness of this "Caucasian savage", as some of the more cultivated Bolshevists described him twenty years ago, and for his remark to a Japanese journalist in 1925 "welcome, I too am an Asiatic." But it is absurd to press his origin too far, and to write, as one commentator has done, that Stalin is "the symbol of the greatness, the cruelty and the power of Asia which is threatening to hurl itself at the throat of Europe". It is probable that much more important than Stalin's ancestry is his wholehearted acceptance of Marxian ideology and entrance into the role of a revolutionist before he was twenty-one.

Stalin's father had expected his son to be a cobbler in the craft tradition of his family. His mother thought otherwise. She supported her son by dressmaking after his father died when he was eleven, and secured his entrance into a theological seminary in Tiflis in 1893. He came there with the reputation in his mother's words of a boy "who studied hard, was always reading or talking and trying to find out about everything." But Stalin was disgusted with what he called "the Jesuitical repression and martinet intolerance" of the seminary, and as his reading broadened he began to have what the Japanese call "dangerous thoughts". He came under suspicion by the authorities, his room was searched, a volume by Karl Marx discovered, and at eighteen his theological career was ended. The young radical managed to get some clerical work to support himself and was quickly drawn into the revolutionary group which had sprung up in Tiflis as it became industrialized. It was 1898 when the Russian Social democratic party had been founded with the avowed intention of organizing the proletariat for the complete victory of Socialism. Two years later one of Lenin's emissaries arrived in Tiflis and enrolled Stalin into the forbidden party.

Until 1917 the Georgian remained an underground conspirator who gradually worked up into the inner councils of the party. Six times the police arrested him and five times he escaped, until the police caught him in 1913 and kept him under close observation in Siberia until the fall of Tsardom.

During those years Stalin would do anything and everything for the party from robbing a bank, as in 1907, to organizing a strike. Unlike most of his future colleagues, he remained in Russia except for trips abroad for instructions from the leaders, and had a knowledge of the workers, based on personal experience, that few possessed. It was in 1903 that he first met Lenin "the mountain eagle of our party". He was at first disappointed at the commonplace appearance of his hero and then captivated by what he described in later years as "the insuperable force of his logic which somewhat dryly but solidly took possession of the audience". Stalin subscribed completely to the Lenin theories of party tactics that had caused the split between Bolshevist and Menshevist two years earlier. By 1911 he was sufficiently valued to be transferred to St. Petersburg and commissioned as chief agent between the leaders abroad and the six Bolshevist members of the Duma. Unhappily, one of these was a police spy and it was he who engineered Stalin's arrest and effective imprisonment in 1913.

When the provisional government of March 1917 decreed the freedom of all political exiles, Stalin hastened back to the capital ready to serve the party but, like most of the exiles, uncertain as to what was the best course of action. It seems that he was willing before the return of Lenin to support the new coalition government, to endeavour to push it more to the left and work with their rivals the Menshevists. This policy Lenin fiercely denounced as soon as he got back from Switzerland, censuring those old Bolshevists who clung to "A formula unintelligently learned instead of studying the peculiar nature of the new and living reality". Stalin at once accepted his master's views and like Trotsky, a recent convert from the Menshevists, worked for the second revolution.

The three men were at the very centre of the conspiracy and when the first attempt failed in July and Trotsky was imprisoned and Lenin had to go into hiding, it was Stalin who kept the revolutionary group intact and bided his time. When the second attempt succeeded Trotsky was most in the public eye because of his chairmanship of the Petrograd soviet and active leadership. Yet it was to see Stalin that Lenin hastened from his hiding place when word came that the revolt had begun. Though Stalin was content to remain modestly in the background as the "hall sweeper" of the revolution and his office of commissar of nationalities seemed a minor one, he was high in the party council. For four years the Bolshevists had to face civil war, intervention and war with Poland. In those years as War Commissar Trotsky loomed large upon the stage. He did not conceal his contempt for this crude mediocrity from the Caucasus, while Stalin was exasperated by the exhibitionism and patronizing attitude of his colleague. Lenin, who valued and needed them both, kept them working in double harness but with great difficulty. Trotsky grumbled that Stalin would not obey orders on the various fronts where he served, while Stalin retorted that he was being made a specialist in "cleaning out the dirty stables of the war department". The way had been paved for the feud which was to make Trotsky an embittered exile stirring up resistance to the Soviet government, and Stalin a suspicious despot sniffing treason in every breath of opinion in Moscow.

When peace returned to the exhausted land and Lenin had forced his party to compromise with the peasant and small middleman in his New Economic Policy, Stalin looked round for a more permanent position. He still held Lenin's confidence ("Lenin trusts Stalin, Stalin trusts no one" was a common remark in 1922) and secured the post of party secretary. This gave him an opportunity to build up a machine which would have done credit to any political organizer, to make his friends regional secretaries and to double and treble the central party committee. Lenin was stricken by his illness at this time and only realized when it was too late the shift in the party position. He warned his friends, with an obvious allusion to the Stalin-Trotsky feud, that "spitefulness in general plays the worst possible role in politics," but he was too ill to take any decisive step and could only leave behind him a political testament to be opened and read at the first party congress after his death. This document warned the party of the danger inherent in a split, characterized Trotsky as an able leader who was too conceited and too immersed in his own work, and expressed doubts whether Stalin would always use the great power he held with proper caution. The final paragraph advised the selection of another party secretary "more patient, more loyal, more polite, and more attentive to comrades, less capricious, etc." Lenin died in January 1924, and, by a stroke of fate Trotsky was ill and absent in the Caucasus. He was deceived as to the time of the funeral so did not return to share in the great display of grief in which Stalin and his allies, the bosses of Petrograd and Moscow, Zinoviev and Kamenev, played a prominent part. His absence was resented and the belief that Lenin and Stalin had remained the best of friends was fostered by the wholesale distribution of a picture of the two men sitting in a warm and friendly conversation. When the thirteenth party congress met in May 1924, its personnel had been carefully scrutinized and only a small committee heard Lenin's testament. Stalin offered to resign but was at once reinstated as secretary. The machine was safe.

Trotsky remained in the political bureau but knew that his influence was being undermined. Unwisely he regarded Zinoviev and Kamenev as his more dangerous opponents and struck out at them in a pamphlet, published on the seventh anniversary of the revolution, exposing the feeble role played by the two men. In revenge they secured Trotsky's dismissal from his post as Commissar of War. Then the triumvirate began to quarrel among themselves on policy. Stalin favoured going slow in socializing Russia, wished to "soft pedal" world revolution and temporarily let the abler peasant become a petty capitalist. Zinoviev and Kamenev turned to Trotsky for advice and boldly attacked the Georgian in the summer of 1926 and the spring of 1927. In a manifesto five hundred Old Bolshevists bitterly criticized his handling of the revolutionary situation in China, where Chiang Kai-shek had just broken with the Communists, and "the petty middle-class theory of 'Socialism in a single state', a phrase of Stalin's which has nothing in common with Marxism and Leninism". Stalin with the help of moderate men like Tomsky, Rykov and Bukharin, all high in party favour, smashed what was called the opposition, expelled Trotsky from the party and sent him into exile in Central Asia early in 1928. Still the opposition continued, though in an underground fashion, so Trotsky was expelled from the country in 1929 and Zinoviev and Kamenev forced to recant their heresies. By this time the first Five Year Plan, which contained a good many of Trotsky's early ideas, had been launched. In its harsh treatment of the peasants and rapid pace of industrialization it shocked the right wing of the party which had helped to dethrone Trotsky and they too began to quarrel with the party secretary. Thus Bukharin, the most recent victim of the purges, wrote to his former opponent Kamenev, "This man is an unprincipled plotter whose chief aim is to stay in power. He changes his theories whenever he finds it necessary to put an opponent out of the way." Stalin outwitted this Right wing as easily as he had beaten the Left but treated them less ruthlessly. They were demoted in rank but not expelled from the party. Then, characteristically, followed milder treatment of the peasants as they had urged, outlined in the famous speech on "Dizziness from Success" which he delivered in 1930.

For four years there was a pause in the battle of personalities. The first five year plan was followed by the second, and the country was out of the woods economically. Abroad it was treated with respect, admitted to the League of Nations and recognized at long last by the United States. At home younger men were rising in control who rendered unblushing homage to Stalin; his picture was everywhere. Thus Kirov, the head of the Leningrad Soviet, said of Stalin early in 1934: "It is difficult for one to imagine the figure of such a giant as Stalin. During the last years, during the time when we have worked without Lenin, we do not know of one change in our work, of one big slogan, one enterprise or direction of our policy which was not initiated by Stalin." The opposition seemed cowed and at the party congress of the same year Comrades Bukharin, Rykov, Kamenev and Zinoviev vied with each other in praising Comrade Stalin's brilliant application of Marxist-Lenin dialectics. This uncritical praise or false homage is one of the most vicious features of any dictatorship and is one of the weaknesses of Soviet Russia which most disturbed the celebrated French novelist André Gide during his visit to Russia in the summer of 1936.

The murder of Kirov in December 1934 started another series of executions and upheavals which have just ended. Zinoviev and Kamenev, who admitted "moral responsibility", were first imprisoned, then 18 months later retried and shot as Trotskyites. A second treason trial was followed by a third and a fourth; even the army was purged of some of its best generals. Of the old Bolshevists who seized power in 1917 not one man remains in a key place but Stalin.

The extent and duration of these purges shocked many former Soviet sympathizers abroad, who began to wonder uneasily if Stalin were a living proof of Lord Acton's dictum, "All power corrupts and absolute power corrupts absolutely." Some found comfort in Soviet Russia's blistering denunciations of Nazi ideology and in her loyal support of the League of Nations in the Abyssinian crisis.

In Geneva the Soviet Commissar of Foreign Affairs, Maxim Litvinoff, again and again reiterated his belief that peace was indivisible and firmly upheld the principle of collective security. When Litvinoff fell from power in May 1939, it was a hint that the Anglo-French efforts to bring Soviet Russia into a "Stop Hitler" bloc were facing stormy weather.

Then came the almost incredible news of a Soviet-Nazi non-aggression treaty in August, for which, significantly, the German Foreign Minister flew to Moscow. The shock was felt not only in Paris and London, engaged in warning Hitler that they would not tolerate an attack upon Poland, but in Rome, Madrid and Tokyo, where the rulers had associated themselves with Germany in the anti-Communist Pact. Viewed at this distance, the treaty seems to have been the clinching argument in Germany for a Polish war, since it removed the nightmare of a major war on two fronts, that has always haunted German tacticians. For both signatories the agreement implied a surrender of principles. As an American observer remarked, "While Hitler erased some pages of *Mein Kampf* when the pact was signed, it is fair to wonder if Stalin saluted the ghost of Marshal Tukachevsky!"[1]

But more was to follow. As Poland, bleeding at every pore, fought despairingly against Germany,

[1] He had been shot in June 1937 for treasonable dealings with German generals.

Stalin despatched Soviet troops across the frontier with orders to carry out the sacred (sic) duty of liberating White Russians and Ukrainians from Polish oppression. A few days later Russia and Germany participated in another partition of Poland. Then Moscow became another Berchtesgaden, to which were summoned the foreign ministers of the little Baltic republics, to bow to Soviet demands for naval, military and air bases. Germans who had dwelt in these countries for centuries were advised by the Nazi Government to return to their ancestral country. When Hitler opened a peace offensive, Moscow newspapers were found urging Britain and France to recognize the inevitable, and the German foreign office warned the Western powers that Russia and Germany might consult on further activities if peace was not concluded. How long the partnership of the German mystic and the Slav realist will continue is one of the riddles of our time. That it has already proved an embarrassment to the Nazi propaganda machine, which had for so long pictured Germany as the saviour of Europe from Bolshevism, is undeniable. But the myth of Stalin, the defender of the weak and the oppressed, has likewise been dealt a shattering blow, as Communists abroad dazedly examine the latest doctrine made in Moscow. If Stalin the Communist really has become Stalin the Pan-Slav imperialist, his foreign policy appears more intelligible to a cynical world.

XV

MARSHAL PILSUDSKI AND THE REBIRTH OF POLAND

"Give us Lord a man to set us free
Arms, our nation's symbol Liberty,
Death in battle if the grave will be,
In our Fatherland. But let us see
Freedom for our country—unity
Give us Lord."

THESE lines from a Polish poem written over a century ago well reveal the passionate longing of the Polish people for freedom. They had seen their country brutally partitioned by Russia, Austria and Prussia between 1772 and 1795. Against Russian domination revolts failed in 1830 and 1863 but the flame of nationalism had never been extinguished.

At a meeting of the French Geographical Society in the spring of 1914 a Polish speaker during the course of his paper boldly offered the prediction that in the coming European war Poland would rise phoenix-like from the ashes of despair after Germany and Austria had beaten Russia, and France and Britain had beaten them. The author of this remarkable prediction was Joseph Pilsudski, an unknown Socialist exile who had become a semi-legendary figure even to his own people. When he died in May 1935, the German radio authorities paid him the unusual tribute of broadcasting a special programme which began with the words "Beat the drums for Marshal Pilsudski who is now in the heart of his nation." In impressive ceremonies he was recognized by his own people as the strongest figure Poland had produced since Jan Sobieski saved Europe by his defense of Vienna from the Turks 250 years ago.

A critic has described Marshal Pilsudski as the Orsini, the Garibaldi and the Mussolini of his country. Successively a romantic conspirator, a guerilla fighter and an autocratic ruler he is one of the most picturesque and puzzling figures that the World War elevated from obscurity to greatness. He was born in 1867 near Vilna, of a family of country gentry which was Lithuanian by origin but fiercely Polish in sentiment. Only four years had passed since the Russians had suppressed the revolution of 1863 which had brought prison to his mother and grandmother, death to one cousin and loss of estates to anther. The mother reared her children as ardent patriots and saw to it that they were steeped in the forbidden Polish literature which the Russian censor had banned. Thus when Pilsudski went to secondary school in Vilna he was thoroughly conditioned against the attempts of Russian schoolmasters to denationalize his fellows and himself. Their sneering references to Polish history so rankled that he wrote a quarter of a century later, "Although I have since passed through gaols and Siberia and have had to do with a variety of Russian officials it is still one of my 'dear' Vilna schoolmasters who plays some part in my bad dreams."

At 20 Pilsudski was a Socialist, not by conviction, but because Socialism offered the only organized resistance to Tsardom, with the land owners cowed by the defeat of 1863, the middle class feeble and inert and the peasants inarticulate. He once asked in exasperation after his party printed copies of Marx's Communist Manifesto, "Can a single Russian soldier be killed by that?" At the close of the War when his former comrades complained of his failure to make Poland a Socialist state he replied frankly, "My friends, you and I caught the Socialist train together. I got off at Polish Independence station. I wish you the best of luck in continuing your journey to Utopia."

In 1885 Pilsudski entered the University of Kharkhov, planning to study medicine. He was soon forced out because of his radical sympathies and, two years later, in the same round-up that caused the death of Lenin's brother, was arrested on suspicion of being involved in a plot against the Tsar. The charge was groundless but the court sentenced him to five years in Siberia where, as Pilsudski said, "I became what I am." These years of exile gave him plenty of time for reflection, completed his emancipation from Russian thought and steeled his determination to work for Polish independence. When he returned from Siberia the Polish Socialist party had just been secretly organized in Paris and Pilsudski accepted in 1893 the dangerous post of editor of its new paper *The Worker*. For seven years he thoroughly enjoyed the excitement of producing a secret journal for which the Russian police were searching high and low. His wife was a willing helper in the hazardous task of distributing forbidden literature and in the days when a boyish figure was not in fashion once smuggled to a party centre 75 pounds of pamphlets around her person. The police finally caught the editor and his press at Lodz in 1900 and Pilsudski faced the certainty of at least ten years more of exile in Siberia. The prisoner was housed in the famous Tenth Pavilion in Warsaw from which no one had ever escaped. When asked by officials why a young man of good family should belong to such a movement he replied defiantly: "When Russian princes mounted their horses over the necks of their boyars my forefathers were already citizens. How then can you expect me not to fight for freedom today?" On the advice of his friends he feigned insanity so successfully that he was transferred for treatment to a prison in St. Petersburg. Here a Polish doctor helped him to escape and after a short sojourn in London he settled down in Cracow, the cultural centre of Austrian Poland, which was close enough to the border for furtive trips across it.

When the Russo-Japanese war broke out in 1904 Pilsudski worked furiously to stage protest demonstrations in Russian Poland. He knew (as he said) his party was "too weak, too ignorant and too theoretical" to stage a revolt, but hoped to make it awkward for the government to mobilize many recruits for the war. Hatred of Russia also drove him to Japan where he interviewed staff officers in the hope of getting aid for a Polish legion. Another Polish leader arrived post-haste to urge the Japanese not to countenance such a mad scheme and the plan was vetoed. Back in Europe Pilsudski broke with the party leaders who wanted an alliance with the Russian Socialists for a common front against Tsardom, and founded the Militant Organization. They trained small guerilla bands which robbed mail trains carrying government funds, seized government pay rolls and attacked police stations. This type of opposition persisted after Russia made peace and Pilsudski claimed it preserved "the idea of an armed movement which would have been completely lost without its struggle". The next step was the organization in

Austria of rifle clubs for the coming struggle between the army of the people and the army of the Tsar. To these the Austrian government gave a semi-official status and when war broke out Pilsudski promptly crossed the Russian frontier at the head of a legion. In his words "I wanted Poland who had forgotten the sword so entirely since 1863 to see it flashing in the air in the hands of our soldiers."

By 1917 30,000 soldiers, chiefly from Austrian Poland, had served in the Legions, Pilsudski preserving with difficulty their role as an auxiliary force to the Austrian army. As Russia was pushed out of her part of Poland, Pilsudski secretly organized the "P. O. W." or Polish Militant Organization and privately told his followers "Russia is beaten, now we must fight Germany". In his message to the Legion on the second anniversary of their entry into the War he dared to say, "Permit me to wish you and myself that on our next anniversary my orders may be read to free Polish soldiers on free Polish soil."

The German General staff realized the danger and induced the Central Powers to issue a declaration in November 1916 promising an independent Poland, but explaining that they must continue to occupy Poland until peace was restored. They also set up a Council of State, which included Pilsudski, but insisted that the Legion must take an oath "not only to serve the Polish Fatherland but also to obey the German Emperor as Commander-in-Chief in the present war and the Emperor of Austria." When Pilsudski refused to take such an oath he was clapped into prison and transferred to Magdeburg. Meanwhile the Polish National Committee in Tokyo established Polish legions in France and, largely through the influence of Paderewski with President Wilson, secured the promise of a free and independent Poland after the war.

On the 9th of November 1918, Pilsudski was visited in his cell by two German officers in mufti who announced that they had come to escort him to Berlin and Warsaw because of the German revolution. On his arrival in Warsaw he promptly proceeded to secure the evacuation of Poland by the German forces and to collect his old comrades to form the new army. The people gave him a tumultous reception and he boasted later "the New Poland as its first step chose, rightly or wrongly, a man dressed in a gray uniform somewhat worn and stained in the prison of Magdeburg." As Chief of State and Commander of the Army he could have proclaimed himself dictator but did not. The Allied statesmen were suspicious of this mystery man who had served two years with the enemy and on Balfour's advice Paderewski hurried to Warsaw to reunite the various groups that had fought for freedom. To make a bad pun, the pianist and the soldier were poles apart in their outlook but agreed to work together to secure the best terms possible for the new state at the Peace Conference. Paderewski was made Prime Minister and returned to Paris to plead his country's cause, while Pilsudski remained in Warsaw to guard his country's frontiers. Not until 1923 was the country really quiet and then only after a series of bitter disputes with Germany over plebiscites, a war with Soviet Russia in which the Marshal with the help of French officers snatched victory at the last moment in what the Poles called the Miracle of the Vistula, and a raid on Lithuania in which an officer secretly acting under Pilsudski's orders seized its historic capital of Vilna and created a grievance which left Polish-Lithuanian relations extremely strained for fifteen years.

During this period the new Polish constitution had been drafted by the Assembly with the deliberate intention of making the President a cipher in politics for fear, as one of its makers said, of "the abuse of power by a man whose moderation and respect for law were suspect". Pilsudski knew the insinuation was aimed at him and refused to stand for the office. A friend of his was elected only to be murdered a week later by a fanatical conservative whose avowed regret was that he had not killed Pilsudski. The murder had a temporarily sobering effect on politics but the Marshal never forgave the parties of the Right and retired from the army in 1923, warning his old comrades that great efforts were still necessary to restore Poland again to the path of reform and complaining of the "filth" that was given honour and power.

For three years he brooded in retirement over his own and his country's wrongs. When a government headed by a Prime Minister whom he detested began to tamper with army appointments to the disadvantage of his friends, Pilsudski decided it was time to strike. On May 12, 1926, he marched on Warsaw and after a dramatic interview with the President, who refused to dismiss the Ministry, seized power by force in a three days' struggle. Then the old Marshal amazed every one by retaining the existing Parliament and refusing to accept his election as President. In his place a chemist, Professor Moscicki, was installed, whom wits referred to as Poland's "unknown civilian".

Until his death nine years later Pilsudski was the master of Poland. Most of the time he remained in the background as Minister of War and Inspector General of the army. Ill health and a dislike rare among dictators for the limelight kept him out of the public eye. He had no gift for administration and encouraged his army friends to form the various governments known as the Colonel's Cabinets. His rule was well called

"Dictatorship by Proxy". He never abolished opposition parties although he poured unprintable abuse upon Parliament and arrested their chief leaders before the elections of 1930. The army was his great pride and always received preferred treatment. Pilsudski died as he lived, a gruff, warm-hearted, bad-tempered militarist who in the words of an ancient chronicler "durst do good and durst do evil too". Like Cromwell he preferred to cut the Gordian knot of government with the sword, only to discover like him that the severed pieces must be spliced together again. With his death Poland entered an anxious period in her history.

For four years Poland watched uneasily the emergence of an armed Germany, taking such comfort as she could from the ten-year non-aggression treaty of 1934 that Hitler had offered her. Colonel Beck, her foreign minister, pursued a devious policy, which even profited in the Munich agreements at the expense of her hapless neighbour, Czechoslovakia. Another former colleague of Pilsudski in the days of the Legions, Marshal Smigly-Rydz, took over the task of training the Polish army, which he described as the "national glue".

When the Nazi leaders in the spring of 1939 proceeded to apply the same methods of blustering and bullying which had been used successfully against Austria, Czechoslovakia and Lithuania, the Poles refused to bow the knee. They took heart from the reaffirmation of the French alliance, and the offer of a British guarantee. Remembering the struggles with Russia in 1920, they were less willing to accept full Soviet co-operation in the new peace bloc. For this pardonable reluctance they were to pay dearly.

When war did come the German generals gave a grim demonstration of the effectiveness of mechanized warfare against a nation high in morale, but lacking in modern equipment. In three weeks effective resistance had been destroyed, and Polish leaders fled into exile and obscurity while the heroic defenders of Warsaw held out until their supplies were exhausted. The Soviet red flag and the German swastika flew over a republic crushed like an eggshell between two totalitarian states. But abroad a new Polish government refused to recognize its defeat as final and Pope Pius XII spoke of a "Poland which does not intend to die." The hour has struck for another leader to carry on the fight for Polish freedom in the spirit of Marshal Pilsudski.

XVI

ELEUTHERIOS VENIZELOS AND A GREATER GREECE

IN 1886 a prominent English statesman, Joseph Chamberlain, was visiting Athens. During his stay a young law student asked for an interview, and proceeded to argue the case for the union of the island of Crete, then in Turkish hands, with the kingdom of Greece. His arguments were so cogent and so free from the usual sentimental rhetoric that after the young man had left Chamberlain said to his son: "That man will unite Crete with Greece and become Premier." Over ten years later, when M. Clemenceau returned from a similar visit, he told his friends in Paris that far more interesting than the ruins and excavations he had seen was a young lawyer he had met in Crete. "Frankly," said the statesman, "I cannot quite recall his name but the whole of Europe will be speaking of him in a few years." In July 1917 the novelist, Compton Mackenzie, then on intellegence service in Greece, made his first call on the Greek Prime Minister. Years later the novelist wrote of the interview: "No great man I have met was more authentically a great man in every word and every movement." This man who inspired such admiration from three such diverse personalities was Eleutherios Venizelos, eight times Prime Minister of Greece, who died in exile at Paris in 1936.

From birth to death Venizelos had a dramatic life. When he was born in 1864 his parents had already suffered the cruel disappointment of watching three sons die in infancy. To avert disaster at his birth they resorted to a local custom. The child was placed on a sawdust pile on the roadside near their home, where he was promptly "discovered" by friends of the family. They brought the child to the Venizelos home explaining that it had been abandoned on the roadside and asked them of they would be willing to adopt it. To this the parents agreed and this innocent device, according to the villagers, was the reason why Venizelos escaped the fate of his brothers.

Two years after his birth his father, who belonged to a merchant family, joined his fellow Cretans in revolt against Turkish misrule. The revolt failed and for six years the Venizelos family lived on one of the isles of Greece and were recognized as Greek nationals. In 1872 they returned to Crete, where the boy completed his schooling and, in accordance with his father's wishes, entered the family business. Luckily the resident Greek consul, a close friend of the family, recognized the great ability of young Venizelos and induced his father to let him enter the University of Athens as a law student. There he spent four years and when he returned to Crete in 1886 was learned not only in the law but in the history and geography of the Near East. Venizelos had also been intensified in his devotion to the idea of a free and unified Greece. In the words of one biographer he "thought of Turkey as Cato thought of Carthage."

Within three years the young lawyer had won a seat in the local Assembly and the leadership of the Liberal party. In a country where party politics were so bitter that fair play was almost unknown Venizelos refused to sanction the expulsion of opposition members and told his supporters that "a party should be founded not merely on numbers but on principles, without which it can neither accomplish useful work nor inspire confidence." Persistent misgovernment had convinced the patriot that he must become, as he said, "a revolutionary by profession and a lawyer at intervals". But he would revolt only for union with Greece and refused to participate in the ill-starred attempt to gain local autonomy in 1894. When two years later the Turkish Sultan profited by the preoccupation of the Great Powers elsewhere to chastise with fire and sword his Cretan subjects, and when the majority then rallied to the Venizelos policy of fighting for Grecian unity, the Liberal leader headed a rising to which Greece promptly offered its support. The Great Powers then hastened to intervene, fearful of a general Balkan war and quite ready to sacrifice the Cretans for their own interests. An English naval officer was sent to remonstrate with Venizelos. He warned the Cretan that his stubborness would only compel the Great Powers to use force against him on behalf of Turkey but Venizelos replied in a sentence which epitomized the history of the Balkans for a century. "European policy is invariably the maintenance of the *status quo* and you will do nothing for the subject races unless we, by taking the initiative, make you realize that helping us against the Turks is the lesser of two evils." "Confound it all, the fellow is right," said the officer in reporting to his superior, "and I hope we shan't have to shoot him."

The revolt did not completely succeed but the Great Powers compelled the Turks to withdraw their garrisons from Crete and to accept a member of the Greek royal family as High Commissioner. With him Venizelos was eager to work for good government but unfortunately the prince developed autocratic tendencies and forced the Liberal into opposition. After a prolonged struggle Prince George had to resign. His retirement the Greek royal family neither forgave nor forgot, a fact of great importance when Venizelos entered Greek politics in 1910. This entry was inspired by the request of a military league in Greece which resented the weak government of the country and the policy of the royal family. They hoped to use the famous revolutionary as a tool in their struggle with the monarchy. Venizelos had other plans. He came to Athens convinced that only in Greece could Cretan freedom be achieved, and aware from his contacts with the cosmopolitan merchant class that the fall of the monarchy, which had so many relatives in so many European ruling houses, would have a bad effect in the West. Accordingly, his first speech in the capital advocated a reform of the constitution but the retention of the monarchy. The mob shouted "Down with the Danes" but in a great oration Venizelos won them over. To his disgust, the king had to accept the Cretan as Prime Minister in October 1910. He had entered upon the second phase of his career with the task of creating "a renovated Greece, capable of inspiring respect and supporting her rights". A resident ambassador marvelled at his self-confidence. "This man is able beyond question but he has not a chance in the world. He does not realize what he has to contend with."

The ambassador was wrong. Not only did Venizelos give Greece efficient domestic government and reorganize her armed forces, but he aided in a diplomatic revolution in the Balkans which completely surprised Europe. Encouraged by the Italian war with Turkey in 1911, Serbia, Greece and Bulgaria negotiated a secret offensive alliance for which Venizelos was largely responsible. War began in October 1912 and on the day of its declaration Venizelos announced the union of Greece and Crete. Turkey was quickly defeated and amid national rejoicing the Greeks occupied Salonika. Unhappily, it was easier to win battles than to make a successful peace, especially with the Great Powers interfering. Much to his regret Venizelos was obliged to unite with Serbia in a defensive alliance against their former ally, disappointed at her share of the spoils. The result was a foregone conclusion, but when Venizelos was reproached by his political opponents for his caution in dealing with Bulgaria he replied with a generosity which showed his breadth of vision: "My critics forget the misfortunes of a state which for thirty years has held the hegemony of the Balkan peninsula."

When the World War began, the King of Greece, whose wife was the Kaiser's sister, was determined to maintain neutrality despite the fact that all signs pointed to the entry of Turkey into the struggle on the German side. Venizelos reluctantly agreed to a temporary neutrality but added, when questioned as to the future, that "Not only should we watch for an opportunity, but Greece, like a midwife, will help circumstances to be born so that she may join the Allies." Early in 1915, when it was apparent that Serbia was in serious danger,

Venizelos urged the king to join the Allies and even made territorial concessions to Bulgaria to avoid her joining the Central Powers. As he wrote in a memorandum: "Even in the event of our failure, we shall have a clear conscience knowing that we have fought to free those of our countrymen still in subjection by Turkey and knowing also that we have fought for the general interests of humanity and for the independence of small nations which a Turco-German victory would jeopardize irreparably." Despite the Allied difficulties on the Eastern front he was not pessimistic. "England," he said, "in all her wars has always gained one battle—the last." The king thought differently. "You know I don't want to help Serbia because Germany will win and I don't want to be beaten." Even when an election showed that the people supported the Prime Minister the king insisted that on questions of foreign policy "I think that so long as I believe a thing is right or not right I must insist upon it being done because I am responsible before God."

The deadlock was complete. To break it Venizelos fell back in September 1916 upon his old device of revolution, though he insisted that his rising was not against the monarchy. The Allies naturally supported him vigorously and they were responsible in the summer of 1917 for the occupation of Athens and the enforced abdication of King Constantine in favour of his second son Alexander.

This action placed Venizelos under the stigma of being the tool of foreign interests, though he could not help himself. Yet, when the peace conference assembled, he was in a strong position to claim a reward.

In Paris Venizelos made a great impression upon both Wilson and Lloyd George. He played his hand skilfully and, as one of his opponents said in exasperation: "In asking he always has the air of offering and in obtaining he appeared to be conceding something." So much was he in favour that the Allies invited Greece to occupy Smyrna in May 1919, thus beginning the duel with Turkey and Kemal Pasha. There, vaulting ambition overleaped itself, but no sign of doom was on the horizon when Venizelos returned home in triumph in August 1920. He had been away almost continuously for two years and did not appreciate the war weariness of the country or the unpopularity of some of his colleagues. The first and most curious adverse stroke of fate was the sudden death of King Alexander from the bite of a pet monkey in October. Of that fatality Mr. Churchill has written: "It is perhaps no exaggeration to remark that a quarter of a million persons died of this monkey bite."

Venizelos knew that the Royalists still resented the events of 1917 but boldly challenged public opinion in an election in November in which the issue was whether King Constantine should be allowed to return. To Europe's amazement, Venizelos, like Aristides, experienced the full force of his country's ingratitude. He lost his own seat and his party was heavily defeated. Venizelos accepted the situation with dignity and retired into voluntary exile to quiet current controversy. Greece had lost not only her greatest statesman but the confidence of the Allies.

Hoping to rival the fallen statesman in achievements, the king and his advisers continued the wretched war in Asia Minor only to encounter disaster and defeat in 1922. For the second time Constantine had to leave the country and in rage the new régime shot several members of the Cabinet for their incompetent leadership. Abroad Venizelos accepted the ungrateful task of securing as moderate a peace as possible and at Lausanne played his part nobly. He returned home at the end of 1923, hoping vainly to subdue party passions, but his health failed him and after a brief term as Prime Minister he again withdrew from politics. "Let him go and let us small men govern the country" was the remark of one politician.

Like Gladstone the statesman soon wearied of retirement and in 1928 he announced his return to politics, alleging the danger of a royalist restoration. The country had been chastened by years of unstable government and gladly gave him an overwhelming majority in the elections. In office again the old statesman announced: "So long as I live there will be no military enterprises. We wish to establish the refugees and live at peace with our neighbours." He kept his word and for the first time in a century Greece and Turkey were on friendly terms. Then the world depression cost him his popularity and his government was out of office in 1933. Soon after his retirement an attempt was made to murder him, which the government was suspiciously lax in investigating. In disgust Venizelos returned to his native Crete. There he was involved by hot-headed supporters in an abortive rising in 1935 which had no chance of succeeding and caused his exile. From exile the old man watched King George return and in one of his last letters urged his party to co-operate with him.

Death came to him in Paris in his 72nd year. Some day when Greeks are again free to speak their minds, when General Metaxas, the latest Greek dictator, has gone the way of his predecessors, when the fires of party passion have burnt dim, the nation will do just homage to the father of modern Greece.

XVII

KEMAL ATATURK AND THE REMOULDING OF TURKEY

A PROFESSIONAL soldier by training raised Turkey from defeat and dejection to defy successfully the Peace Treaties imposed by the Allies and, in the words of one admirer, "swept away in ten years the accretions of ten centuries." This soldier-statesman is Mustapha Kemal, President Ataturk, the last name being given to him in 1934 by the National Assembly when it was decided to adopt the Western custom of having surnames. To ears attuned to American slang it sounds very much like "Attaboy", but we can scarcely expect a Turkish parliament to have thought of that.

Mustapha Kemal's parents came from Albania and Macedonia. He was born in 1881 in the city of Salonika. His father was a poorly-paid petty customs official who eventually left the service in desperation to try and make a better living as a wood merchant. He died when the boy was nine and the mother and two children had to take refuge with an uncle in the country. Two years later the mother, who had ambitious plans for her son, managed to raise funds to send him to a school. But the boy quarrelled with his fellows, insulted his masters, and on being thoroughly thrashed by one of them for his behaviour, promptly ran away home. No entreaty of his mother would induce him to return. His uncle suggested that the boy should enrol in the military cadet school and this proposal Mustapha adopted, passing the entrance examinations and accepting the offer of a place before his mother knew anything of it.

In cadet school he was the same bad-tempered morose youth but the work appealed to him. One of his teachers, of the same name as himself, christened him Kemal or "perfect" because of his proficiency in mathematics. When he passed out of the Senior school at 20 the official report described him as "a brilliant, difficult youth with whom it is impossible to become intimate". Although reserved the boy was not a recluse. With a few associates he had already tasted the forbidden fruit of Western culture in the shape of books by Voltaire, Rousseau, Hobbes and John Stuart Mill, and was dreaming of the day when the Sultan should be overthrown and Turkey given constitutional government. Such views were common among the cream of the young officers transferred like himself to the staff college at Constantinople and Mustapha was promptly admitted to a revolutionary society known as the Fatherland. The

Sultan's spies kept in touch with such movements and one of them managed to worm his way into its councils and secured the arrest of all the members just after our young revolutionist had finished his staff course and was acting as editor of a secret party journal. After a few weeks of solitary confinement Mustapha was freed with a stern warning to "stop all this nonsense and foolishness and confine yourself to your military duties", and transferred to a cavalry regiment in Damascus.

After service in a brief campaign against a rebellious tribe, Mustapha coolly disregarded the warnings he had received and proceeded to organize a branch of the Fatherland society. Hearing rumours that a really big revolutionary movement was brewing in Salonika, he obtained leave to visit Jaffa and with the co-operation of a brother officer took ship there for Salonika. Though in disguise he was recognized by the secret police and only hurried flight and further aid from fellow sympathizers saved him from death. For a year he kept under cover on garrison in southern Syria and then manoeuvred a transfer to the staff of the army in his old home. He arrived in 1908 just as the Committee of Union and Progress had staged a successful Palace revolution and forced the Sultan to accept a new constitutional government with the Young Turks, as they were christened, as his advisers. The triumvirate who led them, Enver

Bey, Talat Bey, and Javid Bey were scornful of the claims for recognition by this ambitious and conceited young officer whose presumption in their eyes far outweighed his abilities. This drove Mustapha, while not renouncing his Western ideas, to concentrate on his military career and, as Harold Nicolson has pointed out in his excellent life of Curzon, set him aside from the group who had to share the blame for the Turkish misfortunes between 1908 and 1918. During this decade the Young Turks had to struggle with a treacherous Sultan in the capital and dissatisfied minority groups in the Balkans plotting for freedom with the help of their brothers in Serbia, Greece and Bulgaria. To add to their troubles Italy profited by the occasion to launch a surprise attack upon the province of Tripoli in 1911. Mustapha fought for a year with the forces there against the Italians and was then recalled to help defend Turkey in the first Balkan war. John Gunther claims that the harsh treatment by the Greeks of his mother in a refugee camp during the war inspired his later brutality against them. When the wars ended in defeat and the loss of almost all of Turkey in Europe, the Young Turks decided to import German officers to reorganize the army. Against this "national insult", as he called it, Mustapha protested so violently and won so much sympathy from other officers that the government decided to sidetrack him by appointing him military attaché to the Turkish legation in Bulgaria. Here Colonel Kemal remained until February 1915, bitterly opposed to Turkey's entry into the World War on the side of the Germans but helpless and deprived of a chance to display his real talents. Just as he was on the point of resigning his commission to fight as a private he was recalled for service under General Liman von Sanders to defend the capital against the expected British attack on the Dardanelles. The German was insulted by the firebrand but respected his soldierly qualities and placed him in command of the 19th division. With it Mustapha held in check the Anzac forces in the landing on the peninsula and won fame in his conduct of operations on his sector of the front during the terrible campaign. Turkish papers hailed him as "the Saviour and Deliverer of the capital", and when the British had evacuated the peninsula his old enemy, Enver Bey, saw to it that he was quietly transferred to the Caucasus front where a poorly equipped and disheartened Turkish force faced a much larger Russian one. The Caucasus might have proved the graveyard of his reputation but the collapse of the Russian forces after the revolution saved him from disgrace. He was then ordered to Syria where Allenby was beginning his offensive. Again his superior officer was a German, the former Chief of Staff Von Falkenhayn. The two men quarrelled so fiercely that Mustapha resigned his command and returned to the capital. Enver Bey dared not leave so popular an officer there and detailed him to accompany the Crown Prince on a mission to Germany where it was hoped he would properly be impressed by the mighty German war machine. The journey had exactly the opposite effect as Mustapha addressed highly embarrassing questions to both Hindenburg and Ludendorff about their spring offensive in 1918, and convinced himself on a trip to the Western front that Germany was doomed.

Ill health forced him to take a cure at Karlsbad while the Crown Prince went home so that he was not on the spot when the death of Abdul Hamid brought the prince to the throne. By the time Kemal returned the Young Turks had won over the new Sultan and he was checkmated again. Again Enver sent him to the Syrian front where in August 1918 the British were sweeping all before them. Defeat was no disgrace in the general collapse of the last six weeks of the war but, while the leader of the Young Turks fled abroad, Mustapha stayed with his men, and when refusing to evacuate the strong point of Alexandretta, characteristically telegraphed the War Office, "We must not cringe. If we do we shall be annihilated."

Ignoring the truth of the Chinese maxim "Get a coffin ready and the sick man will not die," the

Allies proceeded to act as if the "sick man of Europe" was at last dead. But the Turk has ever had remarkable powers of recuperation and in Mr. Churchill's picturesque rhetoric, "Loaded with follies, stained with crimes, rotted with misgovernment, shattered by battle, worn down by long disastrous wars, his Empire falling to pieces round him, the Turk was still alive." When the Allies made the supreme blunder of entrusting the Greeks with occupying Smyrna and keeping the country in subjection in May 1919, the prostrate nation turned and fought back. Mustapha's long awaited hour had come.

He had been appointed Inspector-General of the Northern area and hurrying away from the capital before the command could be revoked, he landed at Samsun on the Black Sea four days after the Greeks arrived in Smyrna. With the aid of other military leaders he issued a call for "a national congress to place in action the national forces under the sovereign will of the people." The Sultan ordered his recall but back came the reply, "I shall stay in Anatolia until the nation has won its independence." Constantinople did not in fact see him again until 1920. The National Congress drew up in September a Declaration of Independence, called the National Pact, which renounced all control of the Arabs and the Balkan peoples, but demanded "Turkey for the Turks". Mustapha was made chairman of the Executive Committee. When the Sultan was induced to hold new elections the Nationalists swept the country and a majority of the deputies, heedless of Kemal's warnings, journeyed to the capital to proclaim their principles in Parliament. The English army of occupation promptly arrested forty of them and shipped them off to Malta. Those who escaped fled to Angora which then became the capital, and it was war to the knife between the Kemalists, as they were called, and the Sultan and the Allies. The publication of the Treaty of Sèvres in 1920, which the Sultan weakly accepted, won thousands of recruits for Mustapha and ended the danger of his being overthrown in civil war. The Allies, uneasily aware that their own troops had no stomach for another war with these stubborn Turks, encouraged the Greeks to advance into the interior of Anatolia. Their first campaigns were successful and Mr. Lloyd George, the friend and patron of Venizelos, declared unwisely "The Kemalists are broken beyond repair." Given full powers as a dictator in the emergency, Mustapha fought a three weeks' engagement in August 1921, which sent the Greeks reeling back in confusion, laying waste the territory as they retreated. The Turks were too exhausted to pursue them and there was a stalemate while the British vainly tried to mediate, the French and Italians discreetly made their peace with the Turks, and the Russians readily shipped munitions of war to an Eastern nation fighting against imperialism. When battle was resumed in August 1922, Mustapha told his troops, "Soldiers, your goal is the Mediterranean." They reached it in a fortnight and the Greeks evacuated Smyrna amid scenes of appalling cruelty and destruction. Only a handful of British troops under Sir Charles Harington barred the way to the capital but behind them was the British government. Luckily the Turkish commander was a realist. He was content to win the rest of the campaign round the green baize tables of diplomacy. The Treaty of Lausanne recognized the new nation state which made no effort to regain its lost provinces of Syria, Mesopotamia and Palestine, and insisted upon the forced transfer of over a million Greeks in order to avoid for all time the disintegrating efforts of subversive minorities. There remains in Turkey as a minority only the Kurds, who have stirred up trouble twice and have been repressed with savage cruelty.

Since 1923 Turkey has faced West. Under her statesman-soldier-President who retained outward forms of democratic government but concentrated all real power in his own hands, the nation regained its self-respect and shook off the customs of centuries. Like Peter the Great, Ataturk would make his people western whether they wished it or not.

The hat replaced the fez; the women were unveiled; Western law codes and the Western calendar were adopted; the Latin alphabet superseded the Arabic; and the nation went to school with the President literally acting as schoolmaster for the higher officials. The Moslem faith ceased to be the state religion and the Caliphate, which once symbolized the overlordship of the Moslem world, was scornfully abolished. The "Grey Wolf", as an English biographer dubbed him, could survey a nation which, in the words of a Bulgarian diplomat, is working as "we never thought Turks would work." Like Sir Christopher Wren he could say, "Si monumentem vis circumspice." When he died in November 1938, he left behind him a rejuvenated nation that remained true to his policies. His successor, General Ismet Inönü, his friend and aide for fifteen years, is loyal to the memory of the man that Balfour once called "the most terrible of all the terrible Turks."

XVIII

NEVILLE CHAMBERLAIN AND THE BRITISH "DIPLOMATIC REVOLUTION"

GREAT Britain has had forty Prime Ministers since Sir Robert Walpole was recognized as holding that position. At the conclusion of his biographical sketches of those who governed England between 1721 and 1921 the Hon. Clive Bigham made a composite picture based on 36 studies. "The typical prime minister of the past, therefore, has been born the heir to a peerage, brought up in the country and educated at Eton and Oxford. Elected to the House of Commons at 25 . . ., he had first come into office at 32. At 48 he entered the House of Lords and ten years later has become the leader of a government. He has finally relinquished the position of Prime Minister at about 60 and has died at 70 leaving a family behind him." It would be difficult to find greater contrast to this composite sketch than the personal history of the present Prime Minister, the Rt. Hon. Neville Chamberlain. A townsman born and bred, who knew neither Eton nor Oxford, he is essentially a business man, who did not enter the House of Commons until he was 49, and did not reach his present position until almost twenty years later. Britain being what she is, there have been few of his predecessors who have not had to face the tremendous questions of war or peace. But it may be fairly claimed that none has had more difficult decisions to make in the struggle for security than this dogged son of Birmingham whose lot it has been to pilot the British ship of state through uncharted waters amid lowering clouds of hate and fear.

The career of Mr. Neville Chamberlain is the latest chapter in what has been called the "Chamberlain tradition". For over 60 years Joseph Chamberlain and his two sons have been in the thick of British politics, leaving their mark upon administrative methods, problems of imperial development and questions of foreign policy. Like the Cecils, and the Stanleys, their family chronicle is a part of the nation's history.

Although the Chamberlain family were originally from Wiltshire they emigrated to London and were for generations prominent in the Worshipful Company of Cordwainers or, as we would say, Shoemakers. The Chamberlains were a sturdy independent clan glorying in their commercial record and nonconformist tradition in religion. As Joseph Chamberlain once told an audience "I have a descent of which I am as proud as any baron may be of the title which he owes to the smile of a king or the favour of a king's mistress." It was he who linked his family's fortunes with Birmingham when he went there as a boy of 18 to protect his father's interest in a new metal industry. Before he was 40 he had established this business so firmly that he looked for other worlds to conquer. He found his outlet in the complete modernizing of the city government of Birmingham; it soon became the model city for municipal enterprise. In gratitude its electors sent him to Parliament in 1876 as a radical liberal who was even accused of republican leanings.

When Joseph Chamberlain entered Parliament he left at home six young children in the care of a sister, as both his first and second wife died in child-birth. The eldest boy was Austen, aged 13, while Neville, his half-brother, was then seven years old. Both boys went to Rugby as they reached school age but soon their paths diverged. Like Pitt the elder, the father had planned a political career for one son, Austen. He was educated at Cambridge, then encouraged to study government in Paris and Berlin, and groomed for the House of Commons which he entered in 1892, with his father and uncle supporting him as he made his bow to the speaker. Three years later Joseph was Secretary for the Colonies, a post of his own choosing, and Austen had got his start as a civil Lord of the Admiralty.

Meanwhile Neville had attended a small college in Birmingham, the nucleus of the future University, and spent a year in an accountant's office. At 21 he was sent to the West Indies to supervise a plantation where it was hoped to grow hemp in which his father had invested heavily. For seven years he laboured stubbornly but unsuccessfully to make the enterprise pay, but in 1897 he had to admit failure and return to Birmingham to start all over again. To this discouraged young man of 29, contemplating the brilliant careers of his father and brother, any prediction at that time that he would surpass both of them in fame would have seemed the height of folly. Their family biographer, ever a devoted partisan, argues that this West Indian interlude gave Mr. Chamberlain a firm grasp of Empire problems and attitudes since "the standpoint where Europe is concerned of all Britons beyond the seas is indeed the same." It is to be hoped Mr. Chamberlain does not share Sir Charles Petrie's delusions.

In Birmingham business circles Neville made steady progress, and, like his father before him, turned to municipal politics as soon as he had the leisure and opportunity. He was elected to the City Council in 1910, did excellent service in the Committees on Town-Planning and Health and established the only municipal bank in the kingdom. When he became Lord Mayor of Birmingham in 1915 he was the eighth of his family to hold that office. As can be seen from Sir Austen's memoirs, *Down the Years,* the two brothers kept closely in touch on all political matters and rejoiced in each other's successes. The younger was still almost an unknown figure, outside of his own city, and when his name was mentioned to Mr. Lloyd George in 1916 for a key position, the Prime Minister had scarcely heard of him. But on the strength of his Birmingham record Mr. Lloyd George appointed him Director of National Service with the task of rationing the man power of the country for the innumerable demands of the war. The post was a new one and in Mr. Lloyd George's opinion unsuitable for the "rigid competence" of its incumbent. After seven months of strenuous but unproductive effort Mr. Chamberlain resigned the appointment. This episode may be the basis for the oft-quoted gibe of the Welshman that Chamberlain was a good Mayor for Birmingham for a lean year.

In the "Khaki election" of 1918 Mr. Chamberlain joined his brother in the House of Commons. Sir Austen was then a senior member of the governmentment and became the leader of the Conservative party in 1921. His brother did not attract attention and was recalled by a Parliamentary observer of this period as "a diffident and quite undistinguished figure of the Back Bench". His chance came when the Coalition collapsed in 1922 and Sir Austen, with his usual deep sense of loyalty, stood by Mr. Lloyd George and refused to enter the new administration. The Conservative party recognised the Chamberlain tradition by giving Neville Chamberlain the minor post of Postmaster-General. The new Minister soon displayed gifts of administration that made him a handy man, holding four different offices during the thirteen months of the Bonar-Law-Baldwin governments. The climax was his appointment in 1923 as Chancellor of the Exchequer. Mr. Chamberlain had not been long in that post before Mr. Baldwin dissolved Parliament to appeal to the country on the issue of protection. Writers differ flatly as to whether or not the Chancellor of the Exchequer advised his chief to undertake such a decisive step, though all agree that he ardently supported the policy of protection for which his father had laboured so strenuously at the turn of the century. But the country was not ready for it and Labour secured its first chance to govern the country.

When Ramsay MacDonald's bungling gave the Conservatives an unexpectedly speedy return to office in 1924, Mr. Baldwin did not reappoint the Birmingham businessman to his former office. The breach in the party had been healed, Sir Austen Chamberlain was made Foreign Secretary and to Mr. Winston Churchill went the post of Chancellor of the Exchequer. As a consequence, Mr.

Chamberlain was back in a former post as Minister of Health where he set a very high record for administrative ability and enthusiasm for social welfare. Such a post does not offer much opportunity unless the incumbent has a magnetic personality, and the public knew far more about Sir Austen Chamberlain, the Man of Locarno.

Five years of office were followed by another Labour victory in 1929 when Mr. Chamberlain, then sixty years of age, might well have thought his career over. Fate again intervened. The National Ministry was formed to meet the crisis of 1931; from it Mr. Churchill was excluded because of his differences with Mr. Baldwin over India, and Sir Austen Chamberlain had stepped down to give the younger men a chance. The way was open for Neville to assume the post of Chancellor of the Exchequer. For six years Mr. Chamberlain held that senior post, gradually gaining in prominence as the Prime Minister leaned more heavily upon him for chairmanship of important Cabinet Committees. When the Foreign Secretary, Sir Samuel Hoare, weakened his position as prospective Party leader by the notorious Hoare-Laval agreement, it was generally conceded that Mr. Chamberlain would be the natural successor to Mr. Baldwin as Prime Minister.

At last the post was his in May 1937 and the Chamberlain family had attained the office coveted by all three of its members. The new Prime

Minister was hailed by the country with respect if not with enthusiasm. His qualities of industry, clarity and courage were widely recognized but experts doubted if he would gain the mastery of the House of Commons which great Parliamentarians like Mr. Asquith and Mr. Baldwin had possessed. To date those doubts have been justified. Again and again he has revealed that impatience of criticism often found in a successful business man who comes late to the political arena. It was appreciated that Mr. Chamberlain inherited from his predecessor a difficult situation and headed a Cabinet which had not previously distinguished itself. There were some who expected him to give a more positive lead than Mr. Baldwin, and to leave far less to his subordinates, but more than one was surprised at the direct interference in the conduct of foreign policy which began with the exchange of personal letters with Mussolini in August 1937, and led to the resignation of Mr. Eden early in 1938. So far as can be judged now the Prime Minister had come to the conclusion that a policy of "realism" was necessary in facing the dictators, and that it was time for direct negotiation in which personal contacts in a friendly atmosphere might clear away suspicions and promote appeasement and mutual confidence. In a sense this was an application of business methods to the field of diplomacy, where the technique is different though the results desired are the same.

The time has not arrived to assess definitely the wisdom of these tactics. The outstanding illustration of them was the three aeroplane journeys to Germany in September 1938, from which the Prime Minister returned among scenes of unparalleled enthusiasm to proclaim that he brought "peace with honour". But the policy which forged the Munich agreement divided England more sharply than any controversy since Home Rule. Party lines were cut across completely and the rare spectacle was presented of Lord Lloyd, Mr. Amery and Mr. Churchill agreeing in criticism with Mr. Attlee, Sir Archibald Sinclair and Sir Stafford Cripps. To the Prime Minister's support came such unexpected allies as Mr. Lansbury and Mr. Maxton. Among foreign observers there was equal division of opinion. Thus the great German novelist and exile, Thomas Mann, condemned Mr. Chamberlain as a Fascist while a Chairman of the League of Nations Council, Senor Calderon of Peru, praised him last autumn as follows: "This knight of peace who possesses neither hatred, envy, nor fierceness has attained the highest summit of human grandeur and acquired honour greater than that of all conquerors." Unmoved, the Prime Minister continued to pursue his policy, convinced of its wisdom, as his famous Christmas card revealed, despite the disappointing lack of response from the dictators, and telling his supporters at the close of 1938, "If I had to live these 18 months over I would not change one jot of it." The mainspring of such obstinacy, apart from personal characteristics, was to be found in his detestation of war. That feeling could be noted in his broadcast to the Empire on September 27, 1938. A life-long friend of the family recently remarked to a critic, "Always remember that next to George Lansbury he is the nearest thing to an absolute pacifist in the House. Mr. Chamberlain will take any risk of war in future rather than incur the faintest risk of being firm now." In one of the many bitter debates on foreign policy the Prime Minister spoke of the awful responsibility of deciding for war which he would not assume "unless forced upon me by the madness of others".

When the German Führer completed the partition of Czechoslovakia in March 1939, the British Prime Minister expressed in a speech at Birmingham his disappointment and indignation at hopes "so wantonly shattered". He asked his audience to consider whether the German action was "in fact a step in the direction of an attempt to dominate the world by force." If it was, Britain must organize for resistance. So the Man of Munich was forced to accelerate immensely the British armament programme, conclude alliances with Poland

and Turkey, offer guarantees to Greece and Rumania, and strive for the closest military co-operation possible with France. No British Prime Minister has been forced more quickly or dramatically to reverse his policy. It said much for Mr. Chamberlain's hold over his party, and the weakness of the opposition parties, that there was no real challenge to his leadership.

But the abruptness and decisiveness of the British diplomatic revolution was entirely lost upon the German Führer. He continued to harass the Poles verbally, and to score a costly triumph at the expense of Britain and France in his Nazi-Soviet Pact of non-aggression. This stunning surprise did not modify Mr. Chamberlain's determination to stand firm against further aggression. He at once despatched by Sir Nevile Henderson a warning to Berchtesgaden that "Whatever may prove to be the nature of the German-Soviet agreement, it cannot alter Great Britain's obligation to Poland. . . ." Recalling the oft-repeated charge that if Great Britain had spoken more clearly in 1914 war might have been averted, the British note said bluntly, "Whether or not there is any truth in that allegation, His Majesty's Government are resolved that on this occasion there shall be no such tragic misunderstanding."

The warning proved useless, and on September 3, 1939, Britain was again at war with Germany.

To a hushed House of Commons Mr. Chamberlain said quietly that "Everything I had worked for, hoped for and believed in during my public life, has crashed into ruins," but pledged his whole strength and power to the struggle to destroy Hitlerism. There was the grimness of bitter personal experience in his broadcast to the German people the following day, when he told them frankly that "nobody in this country any longer places any trust in your Führer's word." The recall of Mr. Eden to the Cabinet, and the resumption by Mr. Churchill of a post he had held twenty-five years ago in the first World War, underline the Prime Minister's steadfastness of purpose.

XIX

ANTHONY EDEN, BRITISH SPOKESMAN FOR THE "LOST GENERATION"

IN December 1938, the spacious rooms of the Hotel Waldorf-Astoria in New York were crowded with an audience which gave a remarkable ovation to the guest of honour. The speaker was the Rt. Honourable Anthony Eden, his subject "Democracy in a Modern World". His address was carried by over 300 radio stations on this continent and reaffirmed the determination of Great Britain as she faced the "strident challenge" of dictatorship "to make sure where we stand, and what it is we stand for, and having made sure to stand firm". Despite the roars of laughter which greeted Mr. Eden's assurance that this visit was not even "one-sixteenth part official", the audience treated the young Englishman with a friendliness and enthusiasm which no foreign statesman has had since the days of the Allied War Missions. When he left for home after a crowded week of "learning and looking", as he described it, Mr. Eden said with obvious sincerity "my visit has been many times worth while."

The prestige which this British statesman enjoys in the United States finds it counterpart in Britain. In a recent poll of public opinion conducted by the English equivalent of Dr. Gallup's Institute, the voters were asked whether they were satisfied with Mr. Chamberlain, and, if not, whom they would prefer as leader of the government. Forty-nine percent. said they were satisfied but forty percent. preferred Mr. Eden.

The story of how Mr. Eden came to occupy such a position helps to explain why the study of politics has such a perennial fascination for so many. The Eden family belong to the country gentry, deep rooted in the soil of England, who have furnished soldiers, sailors and statesmen throughout the centuries. Since the fourteenth century there have been Edens in Durham. The present head of the family is the eighth in succession to the baronetcy created in 1672. One of the family was the last English governor of Maryland and his tomb was visited by his descendant during his American tour. Despite its essential Englishness the Eden family has that strain of eccentricity sometimes found in the ranks of the gentry. Thus, Mr. Eden's father was not only a cavalry officer and an excellent amateur boxer, but also a painter of water-colours and an aesthete with whom Whistler once had a violent controversy. It is probably from him that Mr. Eden inherits his interest in art, testified to by his collection of Cézanne paintings and his position as a trustee of the National Art Gallery.

Anthony Eden was born in June 1897, the third of four sons. He was a schoolboy at Eton when the World War broke out, a war which was to bring sorrow and stern experience to his family in common with so many others. The eldest son was killed in the early months of the war, the second, travelling in Germany in August 1914, was interned for two years and when released joined the infantry, the fourth joined the navy at 14 and died two years later at the Battle of Jutland. At eighteen Anthony joined the King's Royal Rifles and served with them in France for over two years. He won the Military Cross and had the distinction of being successively the youngest adjutant and youngest brigade-major in the British army.

As one of the survivors of what has been called the "lost generation" (of Eden's twenty-six classmates at Eton, all volunteered and nine were killed) Eden at 21 left the vocation of arms to study at Oxford. Neville Chamberlain, then 49, had just entered the House of Commons and Stanley Baldwin was a junior member of the Coalition government. The three years in Oxford were unobtrusive ones in which Eden devoted himself to the study of Oriental languages, graduating with the coveted first-class. But he avoided the Union, then as now, looked upon as the nursery of statesmen. Yet the years of quiet study had not made him deaf to the traditional call to public service, and immediately after leaving Oxford in 1923 the young man contested a Durham seat with the ringing declaration: "I am a Conservative, always have been a Conservative and expect to die a Conservative." He was unsuccessful, but a year later the electors of Warwick and Leamington approved of him and have done so ever since. This was also the year of Mr. Eden's marriage to the daughter of a wealthy banker, Gervase Beckett. Besides his political connections, the latter's financial interest in the *Yorkshire Post* gave his son-in-law entrée to journalism, where he at first confined his efforts to articles on art and literature. This connection also made possible his attendance at the Imperial Press Conference of 1925, when Mr. Eden crossed Canada en route to Melbourne.

The first important step up the political ladder was achieved in 1926 when the young M.P. was fortunate enough to become the Parliamentary private secretary to Sir Austen Chamberlain, then Foreign Secretary. The appointment was largely due to Commander Locker Lampson, then Under-Secretary to the Foreign Office, who had come to like and respect the young M.P. He was still an unknown figure in politics and was later recalled by the *Daily Telegraph's* political correspondent as "a somewhat frail fellow, with a marked stoop, and the tired eyes of a student, rather than the arresting gaze of a leader". For three years he fetched and carried, unobtrusive and industrious, serving his apprenticeship. When his party went into Opposition in 1929 he gained the chance for recognition in the cut and thrust of debate denied a minor supporter of the government. The party learned his worth as a critic of Labour foreign policy. When the National Government was formed in 1931 the reward came with promotion to the post of Parliamentary Under Secretary to the Foreign Office, where he was to be Number 2 man to Sir John Simon. The latter's dismal record as Foreign Secretary made Mr. Eden's own efforts shine all the more brightly, whether struggling to find the basis for a Disarmament agreement, mediating between Hungary and Jugoslavia after the murder of King Alexander, or paving the way for the plebiscite in the Saar Valley. A French diplomat praised "this terrible young man who wants peace", and General Temperley has recorded in *The Whispering Gallery of Europe,* that "his handling of difficult situations gave him a great reputation for sincerity and diplomatic skill. Foreigners liked him and responded to the enthusiasm for the League and world peace that inspired him." Even a Nazi newspaper described him sympathetically as one who "belongs to a generation whose life and conceptions have been formed and moulded by the War." Promotion to the Cabinet resulted, as Lord Privy Seal in 1934, and as Minister for League of Nations Affairs in 1935, while European diplomats speculated as to his prospects of becoming Foreign Minister. In March 1935, Mr. Eden was sent to visit Berlin, Moscow, Warsaw and Prague as the British government strove to mend its diplomatic fences, as Germany openly rearmed and Italy muttered about her African grievances. In Russia he was warmly received and when he left Litvinoff, the Foreign Minister wished him success and added, "Your success is ours too." Douglas Reed of *The Times* accompanied him on the journey and tells us in *Insanity Fair* "I saw a man who worked like a bee and who carefully spared his strength to be fit for the job." As it was, the anxiety and the strain of an unusually severe air trip affected Eden's heart and caused a forced rest of six weeks. In the interval occurred Stresa, where Sir John Simon discussed a common European front with Laval and Mussolini, but carefully neglected to raise the awkward question of Abyssinia. That job was left for his colleague, who was sent to Rome in June to suggest an exchange of territory between Britain, Italy and Abyssinia. The offer was scornfully rejected by Mussolini, determined to take and not to receive, and between the two men an antagonism developed which has left its mark upon history. It was the British diplomat's first failure, and one of his friends has recently hinted that some members of the British Cabinet were not really disappointed and had even connived at the publication in a London newspaper of the secret offer while he was hurrying to Rome.

The spectacle of Mr. Eden as the Saint George of Geneva during the struggle for sanctions in the Abyssinian war was worth thousands of votes in the election of November 1935, when the Baldwin administration avowed its devotion to League principles. Almost immediately afterwards came the shock to public opinion afforded by the notorious Hoare-Laval agreement. Sir Samuel Hoare had to retire as a concession to popular favour, Mr. Baldwin draped himself in a white sheet of repentance, and Mr. Eden stepped forward as Foreign Secretary, the youngest in almost a century.

From December 1935 until February 1938, Mr. Eden held that thankless position as guns roared in Africa, Asia and Europe. The system of sanctions failed in Abyssinia and Mr. Chamberlain called in June 1936 for an end to this "midsummer madness", the forewarning of his policy of realism. When he became Prime Minister a year later, he retained the young diplomat, but it became increasingly clear that he intended to supervise closely the efforts of his colleague and even to interfere upon occasion. Mr. Eden did score one triumph in the Nyon agreement over pirate submarines, when the dictators bowed to a bold action presented and well-timed, but only one. In August 1937 came the exchange of personal letters between Mussolini and Chamberlain; in November the visit of Lord Halifax to Berlin began the era of personal contacts upon which Mr. Chamberlain placed so much stress. In January 1938 Italian newspapers were instructed to comment upon the forthcoming resignation of the British Foreign Secretary and hints were sent out to London that, in Mr. Eden's phrase, it was "now or never" if Anglo-Italian friendship was to be restored. The Foreign Secretary thought it need be neither now or never and that proofs of good faith should first be evident in Rome. As he said in a speech before his resignation, ". . . there must be no sacrifice of principles and no shirking of responsibilities merely to obtain good results that may not be permanent." Mr. Chamberlain was more hopeful of good results and, to the delight of Rome, Berlin and Tokyo, Mr. Eden resigned from the cabinet.

After leaving office Mr. Eden showed a skill in political manoeuvring that branded him as the seasoned politician as well as the young idealist. He was careful not to break with his party, nor expose himself too much to its criticism, as Mr. Churchill had done. There were rumours that Lord Baldwin continued to act as his political mentor, and it is of interest that during his American tour Mr. Eden was accompanied by the former's Parliamentary private secretary. Writing in *Foreign Affairs,* a well-informed observer states categorically "Lord Baldwin has rewritten his former political testament which named Sir Samuel Hoare as next Conservative leader after Neville Chamberlain. The name of Hoare has been erased and that of Anthony Eden has been substituted." Such rumours, plus the fact that Mr. Chamberlain is past his seventieth year, might explain the caution with which Mr. Eden received overtures from the centre and the left for assistance in securing the new government of national concentration that many felt necessary to meet the continuous crisis. Yet he did not surrender the right of criticism of policy and did not hesitate to declare his concern after Munich with the condition of England and the need for "unity, strength and sense of justice".

The return of Mr. Eden to the Cabinet on the very day Britain entered the war, caused him once again to doff the khaki of an officer and don the garb of the civilian. At the time of his selection he was serving with his regiment in guarding the London docks against sabotage. This Cabinet appointment may be interpreted both as a tacit admission of the correctness of Mr. Eden's previous diagnosis of the mentality of dictators and as a recognition of the popularity of the young statesman.

But Mr. Eden did not return to the Foreign Office. His successor, Lord Halifax, had shown in his great speech of June 29, 1939, which pledged Britain to resist further aggression and to lead in the rebuilding of Europe, a vision and firmness of purpose that was undeniable, and with which Mr. Eden was in entire agreement. Consequently he became Secretary of State for the Dominions, with the special duty of acting as liaison officer between the new inner War Cabinet and the Dominions. In this post we may expect him to display the same industry and enthusiasm as has characterized him in the past.

It may be that his greatest task lies in the future now obscured from our vision by the smoke of battle. Some day Britain must again take up the task of rebuilding the temple of peace on more solid foundations than were erected in 1919. Let us hope Anthony Eden may then carry on where Lord Cecil and Woodrow Wilson were obliged to stop.

XX

EAMON DE VALERA AND THE MAKING OF EIRE

THE element of chance in history is one which irritates those who want the past explained by a formula but which fascinates the historian. If Clive's pistol had not unaccountably missed fire when he tried to commit suicide the history of the British dominion over India might have developed on vastly different lines. Had Karl Marx secured the post of lecturer in philosophy in some German university, the greatest thinker Socialism has produced might never have turned his attention to the evils of industrialism. Had one of the Governing Board of University College, Cork, turned up at the meeting to support, as he had promised, his friend's application for a chair of mathematics, Eamon De Valera would not have been drawn into the revolutionary movement in Dublin and the course of Irish history would have proceeded on different lines. Chance intervened and "Dev", as he is known to millions of Irishmen, rules over the Irish "republican kingdom".

Eamon De Valera was born in New York in 1882, the son of a Spanish musician, newly arrived in America, and an Irishwoman, also an emigrant, whose family were small farmers in county Limerick. The boy was left fatherless at the age of two and his mother decided to send him home to be brought up on the family farm while she remained in the United States. The family were generous in their care of young De Valera and his uncle made real sacrifices to further his education after he had shown his abilities at the village school. So family assistance and scholarships saw De Valera through the Royal University at Dublin. After graduation he secured a post as lecturer in mathematics at Rockwell College and seemed destined for a safe career in academic circles. To the disappointment of his uncle, who had been an ardent supporter of the Land League, he took no interest in politics, and his great enthusiasm, apart from mathematics and chess, was the study of the Irish language which the Gaelic League was doing its best to revive. In 1910 De Valera married Miss Jane Flanagan, one of the most enthusiastic of the Gaelic League teachers in Dublin. A student at that time writes of the young couple being "met constantly everywhere that the enthusiasts of the 'Irish Ireland' movement congregated, talking Irish to each other as far as a limited vocabulary would allow, buying nothing that was not of Irish manufacture and taking an active part in all the social and educational meetings of the Gaelic League." Not until 1913 did De Valera have other interests and for them, ironically enough, Ulster leaders like Sir Edward Carson were responsible. They had organized the Ulster Volunteers to combat any attempt to apply Home Rule to Ulster with the rest of Ireland. In Dublin the response was the organization of the Nationalist Volunteers led by Professor John Macneill, but secretly inspired by members of the Irish Republican Brotherhood. De Valera, dressed in rough homespun and wearing a curious deer-stalker's hat, such as Sherlock Holmes used to favour, turned up at the first parades and was soon employed in drilling a squad. Yet he still held aloof from politics and declined to serve on the executive of the organization.

When the world war broke out John Redmond, leader of the Irish Nationalists in the House of Commons, pledged the loyal co-operation of his people. Most of the Nationalist volunteers concurred but a small minority resented being drawn into an Imperial war and remembered the old maxim that "England's weakness is Ireland's opportunity." In that minority was De Valera who was gradually drawn into more extreme views and joined the Republican Brotherhood early in 1916. He was still an unimportant figure and was not consulted about the plans for a rising in Easter week, 1916, drafted by a little group who knew that such a rising was doomed to failure but hoped that it would arouse Irish feeling. As one said, "We expected to be all killed but we thought we should wake up Ireland." De Valera was actually opposed to the rising but felt it his duty to obey orders. He was placed in command of an outpost that controlled the approach to Dublin from Kingstown, and acquitted himself with distinction in the hopeless struggle. The rising was extremely unpopular with most of the Irish people and it is generally agreed that if the British government had treated the rebels with contemptuous leniency the revolt would have faded into obscurity. But, to quote P. S. O'Hegarty, "when Sir John Maxwell shot to pieces the government of the Irish Republic he put an end to English domination of Ireland." The seven signatories to the proclamation announcing the Irish republic were shot as well as the commandants of the various units, except De Valera. He owed his escape to the fact that John Redmond, who had vainly advised against reprisals, used De Valera's American origin to secure commutation of his sentence to penal servitude for life. Thus he had the honour of being the last commandant to surrender and the only one to survive. Consequently when the prisoners were sent to English gaols like Dartmoor they instinctively looked upon him as their leader. It was then that De Valera really began to study the political problem. In the summer of 1917 De Valera, Collins, Cosgrave, Griffiths, and others were set free, in order, as Lloyd George explained, to create a more favourable atmosphere for the Irish Convention.

The Convention got nowhere in finding a solution but the rebels of 1916 returned to Dublin in triumph. De Valera was elected as member of parliament for East Clare to fill the vacancy created by the death of Major Willie Redmond in France. In November he succeeded Arthur Griffiths, the founder and head of the Sinn Fein movement, as its leader, a gesture planned to unite all Irish revolutionary forces under a common policy. The new leader urged his comrades in the volunteers to enlarge their forces and when the world war was over present a demand for national independence backed by force of arms.

In 1918 the British government again blundered in attempting to apply conscription to Ireland, a policy which brought together in opposition the Sinn Fein movement, the Home Rule party, the Labour party and the hierarchy of the Catholic Church. Alarmed at the degree of resistance, the British arrested all the prominent Sinn Feiners they could get their hands on, including De Valera. This time he was shipped to Lincoln Gaol and there had leisure to study the implications of the Einstein theory of relativity. Michael Collins had escaped arrest and it was he who engineered the dramatic escape and return to Ireland of the mathematician in February 1919.

By this time the Sinn Fein movement had won almost every Irish seat outside of Ulster in the "Khaki" election and was drifting towards guerilla warfare. De Valera was greeted as chief of the new revolutionary government and formed a cabinet which included Griffiths and Collins. While in prison he had decided that it was his duty to go to the United States, as Parnell had done, and secure the help of the millions of Irish Americans. Once again Collins displayed his cunning in smuggling this almost undisguisable figure out of the country. In America De Valera had a remarkable reception. He succeeded in raising over $5,000,000 for the Sinn Fein cause but angered some of the Irish-American leaders by his stubbornness and habit of making vital decisions without previous consultations.

On Christmas Eve, 1920, De Valera returned to Dublin. During his eighteen months' absence the war between the Black and Tans and Irish irregulars had been mainly guided by Collins, despite his nominal position as Minister of Finance. To Collins' amazement De Valera proposed his immediate departure for the United States to continue propaganda work. Collins flatly refused to go and his action may well have affected the future relations of the two men. By the spring of 1921 the British government was less confident that it had "murder by the throat" and began to send out feelers for negotiations. It had been careful to leave De Valera free, to the great disgust of zealous subordinates who arrested him and were overruled more than once. In April, Lord Derby came on a secret mission. In May, Sir James Craig arrived from Belfast only to report that after four hours' conversation De Valera had got no further than the days of Henry VIII. General Smuts was the third emissary but found like his predecessors that De Valera would listen to nothing but direct negotiations. To this Lloyd George agreed and a conference was fixed for July in London and a truce proclaimed. Both sides were war weary and both realized that once a truce was established it would be difficult to stir up enthusiasm for further fighting. Yet De Valera rejected the British proposals in the first negotiations, and there was a delay until October before a second meeting was arranged to discuss "how the association of nations within the community known as the British Empire might best be reconciled with Irish aspirations".

De Valera would not attend the second conference and one biographer has suggested that he had reflected upon President Wilson's experience. Arthur Griffiths was sent as leader of the group of five who were given a free hand in the negotiations but were to sign nothing without previous reference to Dublin. The negotiations lasted for two months during which time Griffiths and Collins became convinced that an Irish republic in "external association" with the British Commonwealth could not be achieved, and that it would be best to accept dominion status with powers similar to those of Canada. As Collins said later, "The treaty gives us freedom, not the ultimate freedom that all nations desire and develop to, but the freedom to achieve it." Contrary to instructions the delegates signed the treaty in December 1921, without prior approval from De Valera. He was furious when the news reached Dublin, whether from disappointment at the failure to secure the republic, or from anger because of disobedience of instructions, will remain an object of controversy. He promptly denounced the treaty as in violent conflict with the wishes of the majority of the people and led the fight in the Assembly against acceptance. The debates raged for a month with De Valera bitterly declaring, "I have been president of the Irish Republic. I will never accept lesser office in any Irish Cabinet." By the narrow majority of seven Griffiths and Collins were upheld and De Valera resigned his office.

His party left the Dail soon after to form the republican group. Its extreme members were encouraged by a rash speech from De Valera in which he said that the volunteers of the future "would have to wade through Irish blood, through the blood of the soldiers of the Irish government, and through perhaps the blood of some of the members of the government in order to get Irish freedom." Then followed the cruel civil war of 1922. By the time it was called off, Griffith had died from over-work, Collins had been murdered, Brugha and Childers, two of De Valera's closest friends, had been killed in battle or by a firing squad, and he had been imprisoned. The band of brothers of 1916 was dissolved in bitterness.

Though the treaty party had won, De Valera still held his place in people's affections and was elected to the new parliament. He refused to take the oath of allegiance and with his followers remained outside of the Assembly until 1927 when new regulations made it compulsory for every candidate to take the oath before standing for office. In the period since he entered Parliament De Valera has had five years as leader of the opposition and seven years as head of the government. He has succeeded in abolishing the oath of allegiance and appeals to the Privy Council, in terminating payment of the land annuities to Britain and in setting up a constitution which comes as close as is humanly possible to the ideal of external association which he espoused in 1921. But, as the Ulster elections of 1938 demonstrated, he has made the union of Ulster and Free State even more remote. He was forced in a grinding tariff war to realize Ireland's dependence upon the British market, and to watch thousands of young Irishmen stream across to England for work and opportunity. He has seen the remnants of the Irish Republican Army embark on a terroristic campaign in Britain that has once again exasperated the English people and made reconciliation more difficult.

In his bitter resentment at the continued exclusion of Ulster from Eire, Mr. de Valera refused to associate himself with the leaders of the other members of the British Commonwealth of Nations who stood shoulder to shoulder against Germany. In his own words, "I know that there are strong sympathies on different sides, but as long as part of Ireland is subject to force by a stronger nation, it is only natural that people should look to their own country first." This man with the tall angular frame, dark brooding eyes, and sorrow-lined face, has shown the dignity and passion of a sincere but bigoted nationalist. It still remains to be seen how much he possesses of true statesmanship.

Wide World Photos, Inc.
GENERAL CHIANG KAI-SHEK AND MADAME CHIANG KAI-SHEK

XXI

SUN YAT SEN AND THE AWAKENING OF CHINA

SINCE 1911 China has seen troublous times. The collapse of the oldest continuous civilization on this globe has left a people racked by foreign intervention and civil strife searching for the leader who could deliver them out of bondage. The generation of idealistic conspirators who brought down the Manchu dynasty has almost disappeared from the scene but the memory of one of them is still honoured in every schoolroom in China. A beautiful mausoleum on the side of the Purple Mountain near Nanking contains the remains of Dr. Sun Yat Sen, the father of the Chinese Revolution. His lectures on the "Three Principles" of Nationalism, Democracy and People's Livelihood are as much a text-book for the youth of Modern China as the sayings of Confucius were the storehouse of wisdom for the youth of traditional China. Like Lenin Dr. Sun abandoned a professional career to conspire against the existing government. Like Lenin he spent fifteen years abroad organizing a revolutionary party which today rules the country. Like

Lenin he died before his task was completed and has been used by his successors as a symbol of a cause in the support of which the true believer will fight unto death.

Dr. Sun Yat Sen was born in 1866 in a small village in the province of Kwantung, South Eastern China. His family was one of poor plodding peasants such as Pearl Buck has pictured, who lived in a mud hut, could not afford rice and did without shoes. Perhaps their one departure from the normal was the conversion of the father to Christianity, and his employment for a time as an agent of the London Missionary Society. The boy was brought up as a Christian and buried as a Christian but one of his disciples tells us that his faith was an unconventional one. He looked upon Christ as a supreme revolutionary who "in preaching the kingdom of heaven attacked Imperialism and Capitalism, propagated and practised Communism and exhorted all men to love one another even their enemies." Kwantung, this province so remote from Peking, treasured memories of the terrible Taiping rebellion which only ended the year before Sun's birth and is said to have cost 20,000,000 lives. It is probable that the boy's first introduction to revolutionary ideas came from his uncle who had fought in the rebellion and who taught an evening class in the temple. The uncle told him stories of the fight for freedom and did not discourage his precocious revolt against the memorization of the classics which still constituted most of the curriculum. At thirteen Sun accompanied his elder brother to Honolulu to work in the latter's business. There he learned English and graduated with distinction from the high school. He seemed so likely to become a complete Westerner that the brother sent him back to China at the age of eighteen. It was not long before the youth was in trouble for defacing the village idol and his parents hastily sent him away to an English school in Hong Kong. There he decided to study medicine and after attending for a year a medical school in Canton, he enrolled in the new one just commencing in Hong Kong. He became its first graduate in 1892, winning the respect of his teachers by his undoubted abilities but acquiring the reputation among the students of being a radical. So ardently did he and three of his friends discuss the prospects of revolution that they were nicknamed the "four desperadoes". After graduation and a year's practice in the Portuguese colony of Macao as a blind for his schemes, he and his friends organized an association for Constitutional reform with the slogan "Divine Right does not last forever." Their hope then was that the alien Manchu dynasty which had governed China since the middle of the Seventeenth Century might be overthrown and the Ming dynasty restored with democratic government. The easy defeat of China by Japan in 1894 encouraged the conspirators to plan a rising and they proceeded to smuggle arms into Canton. The plot was discovered, several of the group were arrested and executed, and Dr. Sun only escaped by being let down in a basket over the city wall. The Manchu government offered a large reward for his arrest and the young doctor had to take refuge in Japan. For three years he wandered from Japan to Honolulu to the United States and to Europe, endeavouring to convert the groups of emigrant Chinese to a revolutionary program and broadening his knowledge of Western government and economics. It was during this time that Dr. Sun became acquainted with the Henry George single-tax scheme which appeared in his Three Principles. In his travels he became acquainted with several prominent European Socialists including the son-in-law of Marx. It was during this journey that he was kidnapped in London by agents of the Chinese Legation who brought him there for return to China and certain death. Had it not been for a compassionate English servant, who carried a message to one of his former medical professors, Sir James Cantlie, his career would have been ended. But Sir James got the British Foreign Office to protest and after a direct request from Lord Salisbury the physician was freed.

Naturally this romantic episode became widely known and strengthened his prestige.

When Dr. Sun returned to Japan in 1898 he had only a hundred followers among the ten thousand Chinese emigrants there. Most of these he dismissed as having "no convictions and no deep-rooted beliefs". But the failure of a brief reform movement in China the same year, when the young Emperor was overruled by the Empress Dowager, the humiliation of the Boxer rebellion in which a mad display of anti-foreign feeling secretly encouraged by the court brought severe punishment from the Great Powers, began to bring more and more of the student and commercial classes over to the cause of revolution. Another attempt at a rising in 1900 failed, but in the next decade the Chinese in Japan, Singapore, the Dutch East Indies, French Indo China, Honolulu and the United States and Europe were brought by degrees into a revolutionary federation which levied contributions from its branches. As leader and reformer of this federation, one writer estimated that Dr. Sun raised about $2,500,000 for revolutionary activities during his years of agitation. All who met him were impressed by his enthusiasm, sincerity and tremendous energy.

Meanwhile the Manchus tardily promised to transform China into a modern state, but their half-hearted attempts carried little conviction. As in Russia each suppression of a revolutionary group only resulted in the formation of others with greater zeal. In 1911 an unexpected series of isolated revolts revealed such listless support for the old régime from the army and the governing classes that the revolutionary leaders in China were emboldened to seize control of several provinces, summon a constitutional convention in Nanking and declare Dr. Sun Yat Sen provisional president of the Chinese republic. Dr. Sun hurried home from Europe and assumed office at the end of 1911. The revolutionary federation abroad was renamed the Kuo Min Tang or People's Nationalist Party and plans were made for election to a National Assembly. In desperation the Manchus called back to office a veteran soldier and adviser, Yuan Shi Ki, who still controlled North China. He was an ambitious man with no belief in a Republic, who saw a chance for personal power and took it. On the one hand he induced the Emperor to abdicate in February 1912, on the other, he persuaded Dr. Sun for the sake of unity to resign in his favour as President of the Republic. The National Assembly praised Dr. Sun for "this unparalleled example of purity of purpose and self-sacrifice", and it seemed that a new day had dawned for China. The majority of the Assembly were his followers and he accepted a post as

Director of Transport to give the new President a chance to organize the country.

Unfortunately, as soon as Yuan had secured a loan from foreign bankers he proceeded to destroy all opposition to his personal power and Dr. Sun was obliged to resume his thankless role of conspirator. Unlike Lenin, he failed in his second revolution which took place in 1913 and had to escape again to Japan. For three years longer President Yuan exercised a virtual dictatorship until his death in June 1916. His only failure came when he attempted to have himself made Emperor. By this time the World War had complicated the situation. Japan presented her 21 demands in 1915, which foreshadowed her policy of overlordship in Eastern Asia that is now openly avowed, and the country was involved in a warm debate as to the wisdom of joining in the War on the side of the Allies. The action of the United States in advising such a course after she became a participant, and the argument that it was the only way in which China could get a hearing in the West to secure help against Japan, finally won the day but there were many who supported Dr. Sun when he wrote the British Prime Minister "China is yet an infant republic and as such she may be likened to a sick man just entering the hospital of constitutionalism." At this time South China broke away from Peking with Dr. Sun as its Chief Executive.

For the next seven years he was involved in a wretched round of plot and counter-plot that sent him back and forth between Canton and Shanghai alternately as nominal leader and disgruntled cast-off. The war lords of the South never shook the faith of the students and the workers in the sincerity of Dr. Sun but they were able to block his reforms and drive him from office on more than one occasion. While in exile from Canton in 1923 Dr. Sun met the Soviet Minister to China and found in him a sympathizer with his cause who seemed prepared to help. His early admiration for the west had waned because of its apparent indifference to the woes of China. As he remarked to a friend, "The Republic is my child. It is in danger of drowning. I am trying to keep it afloat and we are being swept down the river. I call for help to England and America. They stand on the bank and jeer at me. Then comes a Russian straw. Drowning I clutch at it. England and America are on the bank, shout at me on no account to clutch at that straw. But do they help me? No. I know it is a straw, better that than nothing."

With Russian help Dr. Sun reorganized the Kuo Min Tang along the lines of the Russian Communist party. One of his assistants, Chiang Kai-shek—now ruler of China—spent a few months in Moscow and on his return headed a military academy where were trained the young officers who led the triumphant march northward between 1926 and 1928. Chinese Communists were allowed to enter the party, Dr. Sun believing rather naively that a study of his "third principle", which denounced the theory of class war, would convert them from their original beliefs. His death took place before the fallacy of this optimism was exposed in the bloody struggles of 1927. The re-organized party was drilled in the veteran revolutionist's Three Principles during two lecture courses in 1924. The sixteen lectures were taken down verbatim by his secretaries and still remain the official party guide to the problems of nationalism, democracy and socialism, if one simplifies Dr. Sun's rather confused economic doctrines. At the end of 1924 he went north to Peking at the invitation of the war lords there to see if anything could be done to bring about unity. His friends were dubious but, eternally optimistic, the veteran leader persisted. He fell ill en route, had to enter hospital in Peking and died of cancer there in March 1925.

Shortly before his death Dr. Sun made in his will a last appeal for the cause to which he had dedicated his life. This document is read at every party meeting and is part of the education of every school-child.

"For forty years I devoted myself to the cause of the people's revolution with but one aim in view, the elevation of China to a position of freedom and equality among nations. My experiences during these forty years have fully convinced me that to attain this goal we must bring about a thorough awakening of our own people and ally ourselves with a common struggle with those peoples of the world who treat us on an equal basis so that they may co-operate with us in our struggles.

"The work of the revolution is not yet over. All my comrades must continue to exert their efforts according to my program of National Reconstruction, Outline of Reconstruction, the three Principles of the People and the Manifesto issued by the first National Congress of our party, and strive on earnestly for the consummation of the end we have in view. Above all, our recent declaration in favour of the convocation of a People's Convention and the abolition of unequal treaties should be carried into effect with the least possible delay. This is my heartfelt charge to you."

Chinese admirers have christened Dr. Sun the Washington of China but a more accurate comparison would be with Joseph Mazzini, the prophet of Italian Unity. Each man was great in ideals and wavering in leadership, far ranging in vision and imperfect in execution, unwearying in conspiracy and disappointing in statesmanship. But Mazzini was paralleled by Cavour. Unhappily for China, Sun Yat Sen was not.

XXII

MARSHAL KAI-SHEK AND THE FREEDOM OF CHINA

THE last of our moulders of national destiny has had, like Stalin, to carry on after the death of his leader, and to struggle for the control of his party. He has had the additional handicap of constant pressure from a great neighbouring power determined to prevent the emergence of a strong and unified nation which might handicap its own political and economic policies. That leader is Marshal Chiang Kai-shek, "weak China's strong man", as he has been called, who is now facing the supreme test of his career. We are watching the progress of the greatest undeclared war in history. The Japanese have been forced to pay a reluctant tribute to the tenacity of the Chinese resistance. If China is beaten to her knees in humbled submission for her failure to appreciate the righteousness of Japan's policies in the Far East, as Japanese spokesmen insist is necessary, China's ruler will be a ruined man. If Japan fails to achieve her objective then this ruler of four hundred million people will attain a place in the hearts of his countrymen that will rank him among the immortals of Chinese history.

The career of Marshal Chiang Kai-shek furnishes an enlightening commentary upon the history of his country during the present century. He was born in 1888 near the village of Fenghua, one hundred miles south of Shanghai. His family were farmers, who had by the traditional Chinese virtues of diligence and frugality built up a modest fortune. However, the family fortunes declined on the death of the father when the boy was only nine, and he has said himself "the miserable condition of my family at that time was beyond description." It was the mother who kept the household together and taught her rather wilful and mischievous son, often the butt of sturdier children, patience and self-reliance. Alone among the family she approved of her son's determination to break away from the family's tradition to become a soldier and later of his decision to become a revolutionary. On his fiftieth birthday, in a message to the nation General Chiang paid tribute to his mother's influence and added: "If each and every one of us devotes himself to the cause of national salvation with the same persistence and endurance my mother showed in raising her family it will not be long before China takes her place once more among the great nations of the world."

At eighteen Chiang entered a military academy and from it proceeded as a Chinese government scholar to the Tokyo military academy, where he spent four years. It was at the time when Japanese prestige had risen to dazzling heights because of the surprising defeat of Russia in the war of 1904-05. Those four years left a powerful and lasting impression upon the young cadet of the strength and capacity of Japan, which may account for his caution in avoiding a major conflict with that nation for as long as possible. They also brought him in contact with Dr. Sun Yat Sen, the hero of the Chinese revolution, who was then engaged in building up a powerful secret society out of which was later to emerge the Kuo Min Tang. When the revolutionists upset the Manchu dynasty in 1911 Chiang supported Dr. Sun and, according to some writers, was enrolled among his secretaries. But Dr. Sun had to admit defeat in 1913 when he headed a second revolt against the new President, General Yuan Shi Ki, the first of the ambitious militarists who have so retarded the fortunes of the Republic. Dr. Sun's flight from China for a time ended Chiang's active participation in Chinese politics. In fact for a decade his career was a chequered and obscure one. He spent much of his time in Shanghai, made a considerable fortune as an exchange broker and, according to his critics, wasted both time and ability in the exotic underworld of that city. In 1922 he returned to the service of Dr. Sun, who controlled the government of Canton and had begun to organize his party along Russian lines with the assistance of Soviet advisers like Borodin. Dr. Sun knew the danger of the Communists boring from within but argued that it was necessary to accept their help since Britain and the United States offered no aid.

Presumably because of his military training, Chiang was sent to Moscow to study the Soviet military system with a view to its adaptation for Chinese purposes. In April 1924 he was made the principal of the Whampoa military academy out of which came the nucleus of trained officers that won the victories in the Northern advance. Here, as elsewhere in South China, Russian influence was strong and one of Chiang's most valued assistants was the Russian general Galen, whom the world knew later as Marshal Bluecher, the commander of the Soviet Far Eastern army in Siberia. Chiang's successful administration of the academy brought him into the central executive committee which controlled the Kuo Min Tang.

When Dr. Sun died in 1925 his followers began to split into three groups, on the left a small group either openly or secretly Communist who wanted the party to go Bolshevist, in the centre a group who would work with Moscow so long as it did not interfere with Chinese internal politics, and on the right a group who had no use at all for the Soviet connection. To the surprise of many, General Chiang came down on the side of those who distrusted Chinese Communists and arrested some of their leaders in March 1926. He was wily enough not to break with the Russians prematurely but induced the party to limit definitely the importance of the posts which Communists might hold. By playing off one group against the other Chiang emerged as leader of the party while disgruntled opponents from opposite camps like Wang Chang Wei and Hu Han Min, left Canton. In July Marshal Chiang felt strong enough to take command of the northern advance and, as it turned out, left Canton permanently. By the end of the year much of central China had passed under the party's nominal control and one of the Northern war lords, Wu Pei Fu, had been eliminated. The party decided to move the capital northward to Hankow, where the Communists hoped to have much stronger support from a community that was more heavily industrialized. Marshal Chiang was suspicious of these tactics but had lost his grip on the party while campaigning and was even deprived of his chairmanship of the executive in March 1927. Shortly after, when his troops captured Hanking there were attacks on foreigners and a looting of the city which he was convinced was inspired by the Communists in order to destroy his prestige at home and abroad. The general struck back by launching a "purification" movement which destroyed the radical grip on the trades-unions of Shanghai and won him popularity among the banking group there who were alarmed at the growth of Communist tendencies. At Nanking he established an anti-red government which denounced the rival one in Hankow. Unfortunately for the Russians, new orders from Moscow, which were accidentally revealed by an Indian Communist and were confirmed in a raid on Soviet offices in Pekin, compelled all but the avowed Communists to break with them and in July Borodin left China. Yet Marshal Chiang was still in a precarious position because his army had been held up in its advance and a large section of the party accused him of merely striving for personal domination. He retired to Japan for a time until the growth of moderate sentiment might redound to his advantage. In November he was back in Shanghai and greatly strengthened his position by marrying Miss Soong Mei-ling. She was a sister of Mrs. Sun Yat Sen and T. V. Soong, the party's chief financial expert. Another sister was married to Dr. H. H. Kung, the present acting Prime Minister. The Soong dynasty, as they have been called, were all westernized (Miss Soong was a Wellesley graduate) and were Christians. Undoubtedly the marriage brought Marshal Chiang more in touch with Western ideas, won powerful support in Shanghai, and gave him the help of an extremely able woman who induced his own conversion to Christianity in 1930.

In December 1927 Marshal Chiang was invited to resume his command of the army, the government broke off all relations with Soviet Russia, and a Communist rising in Canton was suppressed with great ruthlessness. Yet the Communist movement could not be completely stamped out because of the courage and devotion of its leaders and rank and file. The movement went underground for a time only to emerge in a somewhat different form among the peasants in protest against the executions of landlord, usurer and war-lord. Between 1931 and 1934 the Communists were able to establish a Soviet republic in part of Kiangsi province and its neighbours that at one time claimed jurisdiction over 50,000,000 people. It was against them that Marshal Chiang Kai-shek campaigned most persistently until 1937.

By July 1928 the campaign of unification had been nominally completed with the fall of Peking and the retirement to Manchuria of the forces of the veteran war lord, Chang Tso Lin, who was mysteriously murdered during the retreat. His son, the Young Marshal, Chang Hsueh Liang, took over control and despite Japanese warning hoisted the Kuo Min Tang flag in Manchuria. Marshal Chiang had the satisfaction of leading the group of

Kuo Min Tang leaders who did homage at the temporary tomb of Dr. Sun Yat Sen in Peking and announced to his spirit the triumph of his cause. The party executive proclaimed in October that "the party has swept away and removed all obstacles by military force and, having passed from the period of military conquest to that of political tutelage, must now establish a model government based upon the Five power constitution to train the people so that they may be able to exercise their political powers and to expedite the handling over of such powers by the party to the people." For the time being China was to have rule by one party only. Marshal Chiang was elected President, his brother-in-law became Minister of Finance, and various foreign experts were asked to assist in reconstruction. These ranged from Colonel Bauer, the first of the German soldiers who helped to train Chiang's armies, and Sir Frederic Whyte, a political adviser, to Dr. Kemmerer of Princeton University, who headed a financial mission, and Dr. Rachjman of the League of Nations who advised on health measures.

Unhappily, the work of reconstruction was impeded by the flaring up of party jealousies, and the rivalries of military leaders who had only joined the Kuo Min Tang to safeguard their own positions. Then followed a round of struggles between Marshal Chiang and Generals Feng and Yen or between himself and the Cantonese group. These disputes have steadily decreased in number and seriousness as the country has come to feel the vital need of unity and to look with increasing resentment against factious attempts to prevent it.

For that feeling Japan is largely responsible. Her attack upon Manchuria in 1931 took the country completely by surprise and found it unprepared to use force effectively against the invasion. Chiang was compelled to rely upon the League of Nations and Western sympathy. Both of these proved ineffective in checking the aggressor and both he and China became convinced that her salvation must come from within. As Marshal Chiang said in October 1936 in a fervent plea for unity: "No nation can ruin us unless we first ruin ourselves." There were many who raged at Marshal Chiang's fabian tactics in evading battle on a major scale, even when Shanghai was attacked in 1932, and who accused him of being merely a tool of Japanese imperialism who cared for nothing so long as he held power himself. There were others who watched the steady accumulation of trained men, the improvement of Chinese military equipment, and the greater stiffness in the diplomatic negotiations with Japan that have paralleled Japanese aggression in China.

That the more impatient group were in the minority was evident in December 1936, when

Marshal Chiang was caught napping for once and was kidnapped in the city of Sian by dissatisfied officers, among the staff of the Young Marshal who had been expelled from Manchuria. Their action, which had some Communist inspiration, was planned to force Marshal Chiang into a more positive anti-Japanese policy. What was significant in the fortnight of uncertainty was the absence of any rising elsewhere while the general was captive and the expressions of relief when he was released. His wife played an important part in flying to Sian to further his release, fearing, according to some experts, that pro-Japanese controlled elements among his associates might bombard the city in supposed retaliation for his arrest but in the hope of killing the general himself. In his diary on December 22 the general wrote: "When I read the Old Testament this morning I happened to come across the saying that 'Jehovah will now do a new thing and that is he will make a woman a man.' When my wife arrived in the afternoon it seemed that the word of God was to be carried out." It must have been a curious scene when the rebels set him free and the general, with his wife beside him taking notes, sat on his bed lecturing them upon the importance of national unity.

No other man in China has had such a record of military leadership, diplomatic skill and political finesse as Marshal Chiang Kai-shek. If China can be saved from the hands of the enemies it will come through the leadership of this strange and complex personality. He remains confident of its future and, as the embodiment of the "spirit and will of the nation", tells his countrymen: "History has shown that the aggressor nation is always superior in arms and resources. But the victimized nation, rejuvenated and reinforced, has always ultimately 'turned the tide'."

INDEX